MW00851360

Acclaim for Brian Aitken's

THE BLUE TENT SKY
HOW THE LEFT'S WAR ON GUNS COST ME MY SON AND MY FREEDOM.

"I read the book in one setting. Stupendous achievement. Searing. Infuriating. Uplifting. All at once.

Brian Aitken has written a searing memoir about his experiences inside a legal system that has lost its moral compass. From the police officers who violated his Fourth Amendment right to be free from unreasonable search and seizure, to the prosecutors who indicted him for exercising his Second Amendment right to keep and bear arms, to the judges who failed at every step to apply the law correctly and evenhandedly, Brian learned to his great cost how deeply ironic the term "criminal justice" has become for many Americans. That he can write about his ordeal with such dignity and even humor is a testament to Brian's courage, his integrity, and his compassion. Read this book."
-- Clark M. Neily III, Co-counsel for the plaintiffs in *District of Columbia v. Heller* and Senior Attorney at the Institute for Justice

"In *The Blue Tent Sky*, Brian Aitken, with grace rather than bitterness, exposes the evils a scorned woman can inflict upon a good man and how a biased court system will work in her favor. A shocking exposé of cruelty and corruption."
-- Suzanne Venker, author of *The War on Men*

THE BLUE TENT SKY

HOW THE LEFT'S WAR ON GUNS COST ME MY SON AND MY FREEDOM.

BEARD
FACE
BOOKS

THE
BLUE
TENT
SKY

HOW THE LEFT'S WAR
ON GUNS COST ME MY
~~SON~~ AND MY ~~FREEDOM~~

BRIAN D. AITKEN

Cover design by Keith Hayes.
Book design by Brian Aitken.
Author photograph by Jenna Davila.

Publisher's Cataloging-in-Publication data
Aitken, Brian D.
    The Blue Tent Sky : How the Left's War on Guns Cost Me My Son and My Freedom / [Brian D. Aitken].
      p. cm.
    ISBN 978-0-9906554-1-1 (pbk.)
    ISBN 978-0-9906554-0-4 (Hardcover)
    ISBN 978-0-9906554-2-8 (e-book)
1. Aitken, Brian D. 2. Aitken, Brian D. --Trials, litigation, etc. --New Jersey. 3. Firearms --Law and legislation --United States. 4. Firearms ownership --United States. 5. Gun control --United States. I. Title.

HV7436 .A379 2014
363.33/0973/092 --dc23   2014947563

First Edition.

To my father and my son.
I hope the three of us can see each other soon.

"I submit that an individual who breaks a law that conscience tells him is unjust, and who willingly accepts the penalty of imprisonment in order to arouse the conscience of the community over its injustice, is in reality expressing the highest respect for law."

- Martin Luther King Jr.
Letter from a Birmingham Jail

THE BLUE TENT SKY

HOW THE LEFT'S WAR ON GUNS COST ME MY SON AND MY FREEDOM.

TABLE OF CONTENTS

AUTHOR'S NOTE

Many assumptions have been made by many people about what happened to me on January 2, 2009. Some speculated that "there must be more to the story." I have tried to answer these questions over the years but, without the context of the full story, my answers usually only spurred more questions. I chose to finally sit down and write this book to set the record straight and to answer some of the major questions raised over the past few years.

I was also motivated to write this memoir so that my son, who is still very young, will be able to look back at this book one day and realize the truth about major events that impacted his childhood and altered his relationship with his father for the years to come.

Very often, works of non-fiction are written with the names changed to protect the innocent.

This is not one of those books.

For reasons that will become apparent at the conclusion of this memoir, I have chosen not to change the names of those involved. Far too often those in power are immune from repercussions or accountability. Their transgressions are not only permitted, but are almost universally ignored, because they are members of the political ruling class and are, by default, above the law.

I have taken great care to portray the individuals in this book as fairly and accurately as possible. I scoured well over a thousand pages of transcripts, motions, letters, documents, emails, and video to ensure the truth prevailed. As readers will notice, the truth did not always do favors for me, my family, or those who I consider complicit in the crimes described in this book. But that is the nature of the truth.

The manuscript has been read by multiple lawyers and individuals familiar with the facts in order to make sure no exaggerations were made and no one was cast in an unfair light. At times, it was an incredibly difficult task to set aside my own personal feelings towards certain individuals, but the unflattering truth is paramount in my story. Without it, my cautionary tale is worthless.

There is only one absolute defense to libel, and that is the truth. That is what I have written and, since no one else will hold certain individuals accountable for their actions, I have held them accountable within these pages.

Brian D. Aitken

July 26, 2014

CHAPTER ONE

For a second I thought I might be able to make a run for it.

The guards looked up from their cell phones long enough to see me standing in front of them, wearing the discount-rack Hugo Boss suit I typically reserved for client meetings. I had just walked into the holding area behind a courtroom at the Burlington County Superior Court in Mt. Holly—the seat of one of the Garden State's oldest counties.

"Hey, no lawyers back here," said the guard closest to me before looking back down at his cell phone.

He was just a kid. He was younger than me, too young to know what he was doing, but he was probably just as old as I was when my American dream jumped the track into oncoming traffic. I was twenty-six. An old, beat-up, twenty-six. These were supposed to be the best years of my life but there I was, standing in front of three kids with guns who didn't even know they were supposed to put me in cuffs. It was the last Friday in August and the weather outside looked perfect through the plated glass. My friends from college were out there somewhere, probably getting out of work early to head to the shore. It'd been a long time since I'd seen any of them. Indictments have a way of making you unpopular, and I didn't belong to the group of people playing frisbee on the beach anymore. I didn't think I belonged here, at the gateway to prison, either. But there I was. And in that courtroom behind me was a judge who felt differently.

In the brief moment before I replied to the guard, my mind ran through every possible escape scenario. What were the odds that I could apologize for walking into the holding area, step back out, make my way undetected through the courtroom, past the judge, down the elevator, through the metal detectors, and out the door to the seventy degree heat without being tackled, tasered or shot? If I even managed to make it outside, where would I go? I couldn't go home. What would I do if I managed to make it outside, live my life on the run? No, that was stupid. I wasn't going to throw everything away and live the rest of my life looking over my shoulder.

"I'm not a lawyer," I told them. The time for running had come and gone a long time ago. "I was just sentenced to seven years in prison."

The guards all jumped up out of their folding chairs, realizing they were dealing with a convicted felon, and hoping no one caught them ignoring me back there. They traded my tie, jacket, and cufflinks for handcuffs and a ride down the elevator to Processing. After those handcuffs tightened around my wrists, I couldn't hear a thing. The world was muffled and I was deaf for my walk through the subterranean concrete corridor that led to my new home.

Processing was a morgue for the living. It was the first stop for people whose lives had just ended, sentenced in the oak-paneled courtroom above, to God knows how many years for God knows what. I looked around at the living-dead around me. If this was my morgue, then my sentencing hearing was my funeral: a last goodbye from my family, the screams of a heart-wrecked mother, and a final end to almost two years of suffering.

Just minutes before walking into that back room I was sentenced to seven years in prison with a mandatory minimum of three years before I'd be eligible for parole. My life was over and the world kept moving on without me.

For the next one-hundred and sixteen days, I journeyed through New Jersey's underground society of the destitute and criminal. I was moved from a holding cell at the Burlington County Jail, to the rat-infested Central Reception and Assignment Facility (CRAF)—where the guards were more violent than my fellow inmates—and then on to Mid-State Correctional where I was surrounded by a cast of characters straight out of *Oz*. White collar criminals, murderers, drug dealers, one of the highest paid NBA players of all time, and an assortment of pedophiles and perverted sexual deviants were thrown in to keep me on my toes.

The first raindrop of that perfect storm fell when I agreed to a cop's request that he had no right to make. Of course, I didn't know my rights at the time. I didn't know the police weren't allowed to use threats in order to gain consent for a search of a car. The whole situation felt wrong, but when the guy with the gun and the badge tells you to do something "or else," well, you tend to do whatever he says. At the time it just seemed easier and safer than protesting the entire situation and questioning the legality of it all. But that concession led to the cascade that swept me all the way to the room behind the courthouse, about to start a bizarre trip through Wilde's blue tent sky.

On paper, I was charged with Illegal Possession of Firearms, Illegal Possession of High Capacity Magazines, and Illegal Possession of Hollow-point Bullets. The most serious charge, Illegal Possession of Firearms, was a Second Degree Felony that carried up to ten years in prison. Combined, the charges read like someone out to do no good. But there was no actual crime. No *mens rea*. No victim. No violence. No one was out to kill, rob, or rape. There was no intent to commit a crime of any kind. I had just been trying to move from my parents' house to my apartment in Hoboken. The charges read like I was a major arms trafficker.

Despite my innocence, I had been found guilty.

Like most other days I had to be in court, I'd driven down from New York to New Jersey with my girlfriend Jenna and her best friend, Kristen. Kristen and Jenna were old friends. They had gone to high school together and then went off to a tie-dyed college in a hippie town ninety miles north of Manhattan together. These were liberal New York girls, from liberal New York families, who didn't understand why anyone would want to own guns in the first place.

But Kristen was a good friend to Jenna. She never took an opportunity to knock me in front of Jenna and, despite her personal beliefs, she drove five hours round-trip to make sure Jenna had a friend to sit beside her while she watched the love of her life vilified for hours on end by an overzealous prosecutor and an enabling judge.

The drive down that morning was quieter than the others had been. We stopped at a Starbucks in North Jersey, ordered our caramel macchiatos, and the three of us continued the two-and-a-half hour drive in silence. Driving to a funeral with the deceased in the front seat.

I had known I would likely wind up behind bars before nightfall. My lawyers had made a last-minute play for bail, pending the appeal I was determined to file, but I knew it was a long shot. Jenna was more optimistic than I was but no one had the heart to tell her that I was walking into prison that day and I probably wouldn't be out for several years.

The motion for bail pending the appeal was denied and the State moved for sentencing.

"Okay," said the judge. "In terms of count one of indictment number 09-03-217I, that's unlawful possession of a weapon, that's a second degree Graves Act offense, I find the following aggravating and mitigating factors.

I'm not going to find factor number three, as requested by the State, the risk that he'll commit another offense. I don't think he will. I can't find that that's a factor. I do find number nine, and I weigh that heavily. That's the need for deterring the defendant and others from violating the law, first in a general way, so that the public is aware that there are penalties for offenses of this type, and second, in a specific way so that defendant will not commit an offense like this in the future..."

I had known all along this was a show trial. Set up, staged, and executed to make an example out of me. As the words escaped the judge's lips, I finally knew for sure that the judge didn't think I was a criminal, but it didn't matter. He was sentencing me to seven years specifically because he wanted to make a point to the gun owners of America: bring your guns to my State and you'll wind up in prison.

The judge continued, "On count one of the indictment number 09-03-00217I, I sentence the defendant to seven years in New Jersey State Prison. Pursuant to the Graves Act, which is N.J.S.A. 2C:43-6C, defendant will have a minimum parole ineligibility period of three years..."

I could feel my mother crying in one of the crowded rows behind me. My father was angry and helpless, unable for the first time in his life to protect one of his kids. And Jenna. She was forced by circumstances outside of her control to become harder and stronger than a girl like her should ever have to be.

They were using my life like a poker chip. Like my life was meaningless. Like they could just throw me in a cage for seven years as a warning to other gun owners. Like I would just sit there, silent and obedient in my jail cell until they let me out. No, it wasn't going to happen that way. If they wanted to make an example out of me, I'd let them. But, I wasn't going to be the example they wanted me to be.

CHAPTER TWO

Divorce.

Everything happened so fast: dating, moving in together, walking at graduation, moving to Colorado, getting married, buying a house, having a son. But divorce? Looking back, it was easy to see all of the warning signs: how angry she would get whenever someone mentioned postpartum depression. How she alienated her entire family. I thought marriage was forever: You make a promise and you keep it. You work through the hard times. You struggle, but you struggle together.

Lea didn't see it that way.

I think the comfort of Logan being born gave her the courage to finally tell me how she'd been hiding another life from me for years. Sure, I'd heard the rumors about her around Rutgers...but I just ignored them. When she finally told me the truth, two weeks after our son was born, I'd wished the rumors were all that had been true. My ignorance up until that point had been a blessing. She kept talking but all I could hear were the deafening explosions of "strip club" and "cocaine" crashing down in our quaint suburban home.

"Are you serious?" was all I could ask, holding my two week old son in my arms, sitting on a couch in a house I bought for a wife I was just realizing I didn't even know. "So, all that time we were dating. That whole time, you were a stripper?"

"I wasn't a stripper, Brian." She punctuated the word stripper and emphasized my name like I was a toddler who had done something wrong.

"I was an exotic dancer." She sighed.

"What's the difference?" I seriously didn't know. I don't have anything against strippers, or exotic dancers, or whatever other creative titles people give themselves in the adult industry, but I literally didn't know the difference. Don't they both lease out their bodies to perverted old lonely men? And what was with the way Lea defended herself? She called herself a "dancer" the way pornstars call themselves "actresses."

She was pissed.

This was not the warm and accepting response she had hoped for. She felt betrayed by my inability to "accept her for who she was." I was so confused at first that I actually tried to be accepting of the secret lifestyle she'd kept hidden from me. I wondered if I should get tested for STD's and if Logan was even my son, but that thought faded quickly. I saw myself in his eyes and his smile. He was definitely a little Brian Aitken. But who was this other person in front of me? It sure wasn't the woman I had married.

The next few days were impossible. Get up. Get dressed. Go to work. Pretend like my wife didn't just tell me her best friend had gotten her into stripping. That she was doing enough blow to kill a small elephant while we dated for two years. Go home. Sleep. Repeat. Eventually, like all twenty-four year old sons who find the American Dream isn't all it's cracked up to be, I called my dad for help.

I confided in him in a way I never did growing up. I called marriage counselors. My parents flew Lea and my son back to New Jersey and offered her a place to stay, in their own home, while we tried to figure things out. Lea had a toxic relationship with her family so she stayed with my parents instead of with her own mother. For weeks she told me we could work it out. I didn't even know if I really wanted to work things out with her, but I didn't want my son to grow up without his father. Growing up, I had seen how difficult divorce was on my friends and I didn't want that for my son. I found three marriage counselors willing to meet with us for free, but Lea didn't want to talk to anyone. Our marriage was over. Lea left my parents' house one day and never came back. I found company with another woman. I was disappointed I'd allowed myself to be deceived. I made poor decisions to feed my self pity and then, after the longest month of my life, I decided to move back to New Jersey to be closer to the only thing that really mattered: my son.

It didn't take me long to land a job in the city as a publisher for an international publishing house called MediaPlanet. In that boiler room overlooking the panhandlers, artists, and crazies in Union Square I produced reports that were distributed in the *Wall Street Journal*, *USA Today*, and *The Washington Post*. I landed clients like Sony, Samsung, and Bang & Olufsen and even took on the role of journalist when I interviewed the head of malaria control at Kenya's Ministry of Health about the reduction in malaria-related child mortality and Pat Croce, the Philadelphia physical therapist who went on to buy the 76ers, about entrepreneurship and his obsession with pirates. The money left a lot to be desired but the commission incentive was strong and I needed every penny to keep paying the mortgage out in Colorado—not to mention the legal fees for my custody battle and twelve-hundred bucks a month for a poorly lit room above a popular sushi restaurant in Hoboken.

For the next few months I traveled between my home in Colorado, family court in New Jersey, and work in New York on a regular basis. My life had become a routine of organized chaos. Some weeks I could only make it into the office for two or three days, spending the other days meeting with social workers, lawyers, and court-appointed mediators. To make matters worse, my scheduled visitation with my son was 90 minutes south of Hoboken in the middle of a weekday. The courts were forcing me to choose: my job or my son. I tried explaining to the judge, over and over, that if I continued to miss work I was going to lose my job and would be unable to pay my child support, but they refused to move my parenting time to the weekend.

I knew how much Lea cared about money, but she had a trust fund to fall back on. What she wanted more than money was revenge. I pleaded with the court and I pleaded with Lea, but nothing changed. Happiness appeared to be a zero-sum game. Lea could only be happy if I wasn't, even if it meant raising my son without his father.

For most people, this would have been impossible. My colleagues at MediaPlanet weren't the happiest about all of my "vacation days," as if I was drinking beers on the beach outside Jenkinson's Boardwalk instead of battling tooth and nail just to see my son. Fortunately, management looked the other way so long as I kept the money coming in. For a while I brought in more money than any other publisher, and that bought me time.

I'd gotten used to fending for myself.

No matter what happened while I was growing up my mom

never seemed too concerned about me. "He's a survivor," she told my grandmother after I was brought back to the house in the back of a squad car for riding my bicycle after dark, "he'll be ok." I was sixteen the first time I was picked up by the police for not breaking the law.

Part of that "survival" mentality just meant focusing on the things I could control instead of the decisions other people would inevitably try to make for me.

I grew up in a town where kids had nice things and families took expensive vacations. My family was in no way poor, but children of multi-millionaire CEO's went to my public school, and we had just moved to town when I was in the first grade from a narrow row home in Northeast Philadelphia. We weren't the only ones. A lot of families were moving from the city to the suburbs back then, trying to make a better life for their kids than they had had.

To provide some perspective of just how wild the wealth disparity was, my mom grew up in the projects with five siblings when my dad dropped out of high school and pulled her out of the inner city. He made a life for himself and his family while the kids he went to Lincoln with wound up dead, addicted, or in prison. "If you want something, go and get it," he used to tell me, "you don't deserve anything and no one's going to give you a thing." I saw those other kids growing up, having everything they wanted handed to them, and I started working.

I got my first job delivering newspapers when I was eleven years old, determined that making $1.25 an hour was going to provide me freedom while my friends played video games on consoles my family couldn't afford. As the middle child, I really had no other choice. If I wanted something I had to go out and make it happen on my own. I learned the value of hard work and determination at a very young age, lessons my dad is still proud to have instilled in me. Like most decisions, working thirty hours a week as a sixth grader wasn't without its consequences. There were times when I would fall asleep in the middle of class because I had been up at 4am working until the bus picked me up. That was just the way things were. I hustled and kept my eyes on the long game. That hustle and work ethic got me into Rutgers and helped me land a great job right out of college when many of my classmates moved back in with their parents to figure out what the hell to do next. That hustle was the one reason I was able to buy myself time at MediaPlanet and focus on what mattered.

Eventually, though, my time ran out and I left a job that was perfect for me. I loved working there. I was able to interview fascinating people around the world, I helped build out the national presence of a global company, and I met and worked with some really amazing people. But, I couldn't buy myself any more time. On December 3, 2008 I took my last commission check and walked out forever.

Out of work and having exhausted over $30,000 in legal fees

from the divorce, most of which I borrowed from my parents, I explained to my roommate that I needed to move out. He was understanding about it all and by mid-December I did what no grown man ever wants to do: I moved back in with my parents.

I was only there for a week before I flew out to Colorado with Mike, my best friend from high school. After being listed on the MLS for half a year, the home I had purchased to raise my family in was finally under contract.

I had purchased our humble three-bedroom house out of foreclosure proceedings and picked it up at a great price. Lea and I couldn't afford the nicer homes in the area, but with a little elbow grease and a couple of home improvement loans, we were able to repair a house that had been left in less than ideal conditions by the previous occupants and turn it into a home. It looked great. New hardwood floors. New carpet. New furnishings all around. After the home-improvement loans we still only owed about $150,000 on a house valuated near $220,000. Unfortunately, the court had taken over the sale of the house as part of the divorce. What would have been a great investment for our family wound up being sold for the same price we paid for it before pouring tens of thousands of dollars into renovations. We were ordered to take the first offer we got—and we did. The buyers were a real estate investment firm who turned around and sold it for $40,000 more than they paid.

It was late December by the time Mike and I made it to Colorado to get the last of my belongings out of the house before Lea and I signed the closing documents. I veiled the trip as a snowboarding vacation, but Mike knew it was more than that. After a few days snowboarding at Breckenridge, we drove the rental car out to Broomfield, a Rocky Mountain suburb between Denver and Boulder, and grabbed the last remnants of my former life: some rock climbing gear, my ice climbing tools, and my guns.

I was a little worried about traveling with my firearms, so I went online to make sure they were legal and to find out exactly what I needed to do in order to fly with them from Colorado to New Jersey. My heart raced when I declared them at the airport but after a thorough inspection of my firearms by the TSA, I was given a receipt clearing my firearms for travel and checked them with my luggage.

On the flight back, Mike and I talked about a lot of things. Neither of us had skied out west before and we were pretty excited about how much better riding in the Rockies was compared to the icy hills of the Poconos and Vermont. We talked about taking the LSAT and going to law school, something I mentioned to him almost daily. I told him how much it sucked living back at my parents' house. Mike had a massive two-bedroom apartment in Hoboken, a great view of the Empire State Building, and no roommates. He agreed to ask his parents if they would be ok with me moving in temporarily, rent free, while I figured things out. Within seventy-two hours he called me to ask if I could move in on the first.

After going through the hassle of moving all of my things out of Hoboken there I was, moving everything back just a few weeks later.

Things were off to a good start on the first Friday of January, 2009. I'd only been back from Colorado for a few days, and had spent most of the previous day moving furniture back up to Hoboken, but I still had enough of my belongings left at my parents' house to fill my Honda Civic. Mike and I talked about getting a bucket of Nuclear BBQ wings from Cluck U Chicken and a few beers after I was done moving in, and it looked like the house was going to sell in the next couple of weeks.

My plan for the weekend was pretty straightforward: On Friday, I would drive down to my parents' house, get the last of my belongings, and drive back up to the new apartment. A few friends wanted to get together on Saturday to welcome me back to the neighborhood, and then Sunday I'd drive down to Toms River to see my son. I could no longer afford my lawyer, but she was finally able to move my visitation to the weekend before she stopped representing me.

Unfortunately, the Parenting Time Order was worthless. Lea simply ignored it. Sometimes I'd show up to see my son and he would just never arrive. No explanation. No apologies.

No phone calls or text messages. I would just sit there, wondering if there had been a car accident or something. I called local hospitals to see if anyone brought in a young child matching Logan's description. Hours later, sitting in the dark outside the library—where Lea was supposed to meet me to drop off our son—I'd get a text message letting me know everything was "fine" and to "leave her alone." Just a week earlier my family and I waited around for hours on Christmas to see my son, but she never brought him. All I had was a worthless piece of paper signed by a Judge. She knew it was worthless and acted with complete impunity.

That morning, as I drove down the Turnpike to my parents' house, she sent the latest news via text message:

> "Have to cancel for Sunday. Lawyer says it's fine. Don't call."

Lea wanted to hurt me. She knew the only reason I was back in New Jersey was to be closer to my son. She knew I didn't forgive her for how she had deceived me for so long, and I think my inability to fully forgive her led to the kind of wrath that only a scorned woman knows. I can only imagine the pain she felt when I decided to move on and spend time with other people. I know she was heartbroken, and I was too, but the person I pained for no longer existed.

Her pain led her to do lots of things I never saw coming. I suppose I was naïve to think we could just split everything down the middle and move on like mature adults. Instead, she fabricated stories that I had been physically abusive to her and my two-month old son. The allegations included virtually every straw an angered mother could grasp in her desperation to inflict mortal wounds to a new father who loved his son but could no longer love her.

That text, I realize now, was a tipping point in my life. Things were never going to go back to the way they were, and from that moment forward life would be different in every conceivable way.

The optimism I had always been known for was being replaced with a dark cynicism, and my friends were starting to worry about how the divorce was impacting me. Some girls, with lip-glossed ulterior motives of their own, told me to just forget about my son and walk away. One of my best friends told me how difficult his childhood had been because his parents went through a hostile divorce. He recommended I just give Lea space and let her cool down. "Besides," he assured me, "kids don't really remember much before they're five years old anyway."

But I wasn't ready to give up on my son.

I picked up my phone and called my mom. I should have waited until I was more level headed—until I had a chance to cool down—but I was desperate, and didn't know what else to do or who else to call. I felt like if I didn't act now this cycle of alienation would just continue forever.

"She's canceling again," I said as my mom answered the phone, far too pissed off to even say "hi" to my own mother. All I heard on the other end of the line was a retreating sigh of defeat. "Hello? Mom, are you there?"

The call was short. Maybe a minute or two. Just enough time to tell my mom that this wasn't just about me seeing my son; it was about her being able to see her grandson, too. I was out of cash and desperate to find a way to retain a lawyer, but my parents had invested heavily in real estate and we were just entering the second dip of the most recent recession. They were trying to keep their investments from going under, and had their own problems to worry about.

"I'm sorry, Brian. There's nothing we can do."

I hung up the phone and tossed it on the passenger seat. It was one thing to give up on me, a grown man. But how could they turn their backs on their own grandson? These weren't the same fight-to-the-death parents who had raised me. They were worn down from a recession that had hit them especially hard. They were also just starting to crawl out from under the pain of my brother's decade of suicide threats, and my mothers addiction to painkillers and wine— the preferred mixer for suburban mothers who simply can't deal with "it" anymore. My failings as a man unable to keep his family together were just too much for them to handle. I was on my own.

As I pulled up to my childhood home, I thought of what I

needed to grab from my old bedroom and the most efficient way to get everything from the house and into my car. I didn't want to spend any more time there than I had to.

One box, duffel bag, and backpack at a time, I loaded the last of my earthly possessions into my car. My book collection, clothes, hand-me-down dishware that got me through college, along with pots and pans and over sixty pounds of rock and ice climbing gear crammed into my Honda Civic from floor to ceiling.

I made one last trip into my parents' house, trying unsuccessfully to ignore my mom's excuses for being unable to help. No matter how logical or pragmatic her reasons were, I didn't care. No excuse was good enough for giving up on my son. I grabbed one last duffel bag from my bedroom, looked my mother in the eyes, and asked rhetorically, "What the fuck's the point of being here if I can't even see my son?" He was the entire reason I left the Rockies in the first place.

Famous last words.

I was too angry to realize I was being a selfish jerk, or that my words might be misinterpreted. For years, I had thought my parents had it all. The beach houses in Ocean City and the shiny the new cars. They had all of the trappings of a happy and successful family. For reasons I still don't know they never told me about the problems they were having with my brother or my mom's battle to maintain sobriety. I thought that they had the means to help but chose not to.

With that last duffel bag locked away in the trunk, I drove off for Hoboken.

I wasn't on the road for more than a half hour before my phone rang.

"This is Brian," I answered.

"Hey Brian, this is Officer Joy from the Mount Laurel Police Department. We responded to an abandoned 9-1-1 call at your parents house..." I tuned out, trying to simultaneously concentrate on navigating the Turnpike's northbound traffic and figure out why the police were calling me. In the background, I heard him asking questions about what happened and where I was but I don't remember answering.

"Would you mind coming back to your parent's house?" I heard him ask as I snapped back to reality.

"Why would I come back? Do I have to?"

"Well, any time we get a domestic call, we get worried about people. We just want to talk to you, check you for bruises, make sure you weren't assaulted or anything, that's all."

I chose my words carefully and honestly. I explained that my soon-to-be ex-wife had been keeping my son from me and that I was upset. He asked if I was suicidal and I answered honestly: No. I didn't even know where he'd gotten that idea from until I remembered what I'd said to my mom on the way out the door:

"What the fuck's the point of being here if I can't even see my son?"

My mom, who worked for the Burlington County Family Support Organization (BCFSO), had called 9-1-1 thinking those words might have meant I was suicidal. Years of training, workshops, and meeting families in the emergency room to help them cope with their teenagers recent suicide attempt had been engrained in her. Her fingers hit the keypad instinctively then, realizing it wasn't some kid with a history of suicide but her own son—the "survivor"—she hung up before anyone even answered. It was too late. The police traced the call and showed up at my parents' house in full force, three squad cars deep.

"Ok, well we'd still like you to come back and talk to us." I heard Officer Joy's voice through my cellphone as the signs for Exit 5 on the Turnpike approached.

"Uh-huh. Am I legally required to go back to my parents' house?"

"No, sir. You're not legally required to, but we'd like you to."

"Ok, well, I'm just going to keep driving then." I didn't know much about my rights but I knew that things weren't going to end well if the police were involved. There was no way I was going to turn around and head back if I wasn't legally required to.

"So you're not coming back?"

"No," I said goodbye and hung up the phone.

That was a close call. I knew I hadn't done anything wrong, but I couldn't help but feel the same panic and anxiety everyone feels when the police switch their lights on to pull you over. It doesn't matter how innocent you are. The guys with the guns and badges can seriously ruin your day.

Relieved, I turned the volume on the radio up and kept on driving... but I didn't get through a single track before the phone rang again.

I took a deep breath and answered the phone.

"Brian, it's Officer Joy again." I could tell from his voice that something had changed. He went on to tell me he had issued a "General Alert" to the surrounding jurisdictions with the make and model of my car and that, if any police saw me, they would "pick me up and bring me back."

"But, you said I didn't have to come back." I said.

"Listen, Brian," Joy's voice said over the cellphone, "there's an easy way to do this and there's a hard way to do this. You can either come back on your own or we'll find you and bring you back."

Nothing about this felt right.

Joy made it sound like there was a manhunt out for me, like I should expect helicopters overhead at any second and if I didn't do what he said I was going to be arrested. For what, exactly, was unclear.

This was not an act of free will. A guy with a gun was telling me that if I didn't do what he said, I was going to be hunted down by every guy with a badge and a gun in the State.

Left with no real choice, I turned around and headed back to Mount Laurel.

Despite implying that I was going to be the subject of an O.J. Simpson-style manhunt, the police seemed pretty relaxed back at my parents' house. No guns were drawn. They didn't throw me down on the hood of my car. It was all very bizarre, considering how that last phone call went.

But I knew something was up when I heard the first words out of Officer Joy's mouth.

"Hey, Brian, Officer Joy," I stuck out my hand but he didn't shake it. "We talked on the phone. Listen, do you own any guns?"

Fuck.

This was not going to go well. They didn't ask me what had happened or how I was feeling. They didn't express the earlier concern that I might be suicidal, as they would later claim. There wasn't an ambulance standing by. Or a social worker. No one administered a psychological test to assess my state of mind or bring me to the Emergency Room.

Just "Do you own any guns?"

"Yes," I said. "I do."

I thought back to the three guns I had packed in that last duffel bag. The ones sitting in the trunk less than ten feet away from us.

Lea and I bought them—a Smith & Wesson Sigma 9mm; a James Bond style Walther PPKS for Lea's personal use; and a Kahr Arms PM9—while we were living in Colorado. We'd made the purchases in 2008 for self-defense, after some nut job went on a shooting spree ten miles from our new home —killing four and wounding five others before being taken out with several well-placed shots from a woman who'd been carrying concealed—along with "home-defense" ammo recommended by the guy behind the counter. A few days earlier I had called the New Jersey State Police to ask them what I needed to do to transport my firearms from one house to another. I had cleaned them, packed them in a box, and locked them in the trunk of my car—unloaded—just like that State Trooper told me to. Now they were sitting in my trunk and the local municipal cops didn't seem to care about me at all. All they cared about was if I owned guns.

Joy telegraphed his next question like a boxer who'd never been in the ring before.

"Do you mind if we search your car?"

"That doesn't really seem necessary to me, do I have to?"

I bought time by talking to them for a half hour. I thought if I alleviated any concerns of theirs that I'd be allowed to just go home, but that didn't happen.

"Listen. Brian. Here's the deal. If you let us search your car then we can say we checked it out, everything was good, and send you on your way."

"Ok, but what if I don't want you to search my car?"

Joy looked like I was about to ask him to show me a warrant or something.

"Ok, here's how it is. You can sign the consent form and let us search your car or I can take you to a psych hospital where they'll hold you for 72 hours on a suicide watch. You wanna spend your weekend like that?" He looked at me for an answer but didn't get one, "you know what happens after you get sent off to the psych hospital? We impound your car. Then we gotta take everything out of your car to take inventory to make sure you get everything back so, one way or another, we're gonna search that car."

I should have taken my chance with the manhunt.

I signed the consent form and two of them tore through almost every single thing I'd accumulated over twenty-five years, while another cop stood guard over me.

It took them an hour to search my car. They claimed it was for "my safety" but they ignored over four-hundred feet of climbing rope and two ice axes, pretending like the only thing that could pose any threat were unloaded firearms locked in the trunk of my car. I tried explaining how I had already talked to the State Police and had packed my car exactly as the Trooper told me to; exactly as the law said to.

But they didn't seem to know the law.

"Do you have a permit for these? Are they registered?" Joy asked, seemingly unaware of the fact that New Jersey doesn't require people to have permits to own guns—only to carry concealed or to purchase—and there sure as hell wasn't any law requiring gun owners to register their firearms. I knew because I had just asked the State Trooper in charge of "firearms" a few days ago. He sent me to their website where I read the law in black and white. How could I know these laws better than him?

One of the other officers seemed conflicted. It was clear Joy wanted to confiscate my firearms, but he appeared worried that my guns might actually be legal.

That other officer was Jeffrey Palladino—a relatively nice guy who spoke to me like an actual human being— and he took the guns from Joy and brought them up to my parents' house. As he handed them over to my dad he said "put them in your safe and have Brian come back and pick them up after things have cooled down."

Crisis averted.

Then the unthinkable happened. My dad came back to the front door; the box with my guns still in his hands. From the curb I couldn't hear what he said to the officer, I just saw Palladino take the box and walk back to the group of squad cars staggered in the middle of my parents' white-bread suburban street.

The guns didn't fit in my dad's safe.

Rather than hide them in his closet or the attic—or anywhere—he put them right back in the hands of the police. Five minutes later, I was handcuffed, placed in the back of a squad car, and driven off to the local police department.

I was booked on the charge of "Illegal Possession of Unregistered Firearms" – a crime that doesn't even exist since there's no registration law in New Jersey. Within an hour, they added two more charges: "Illegal Possession of High Capacity Magazines" and "Illegal Possession of Hollow-point Ammunition."

Two-and-a-half hours after I started talking to the police I was finally read my Miranda Warning and settled in for a long weekend in County Jail.

The shit, as they say, had hit the fan.

CHAPTER THREE

For as far back as I can remember we have been at war.

Just four days before I was born American forces began the fifty-one day invasion of Grenada. My childhood was punctuated with grainy live footage of bombardments in Iraq during Operation Desert Storm. We had playing cards and comic books supporting the invasion. The propaganda ran thick. We supported our troops with ribbons and flags, determined not to repeat Vietnam, either on the battlefield or in the way we treated our returning veterans. As children, and as a country, we became unified by war and played Army, crawling through the woods behind our homes wearing the fatigues of our family members and friends who returned home. For the first time in history we could watch war, live, on our television screens.

The twin towers fell a decade later. We watched from a television in our South Jersey high school's shop-class. Children who had parents working in the city were called down to the office. Classmates who were volunteer firefighters went against their orders and drove up to New York to volunteer on sight. Many more of them enlisted to fight in the "War on Terror." Some of them never came home. I don't think my generation knows what it means to live during "peacetime." We were raised, and continue to live, in a perpetual state of war. Our senses are numbed to it.

We don't know any better.

By the time Lea and I entered into a full-scale conflict with each other America was entering into it's eighth year in Iraq and Afghanistan, attempting to bring "democracy" and "stability" to a region that's known conflict for thousands of years. Lea and I were at war with each other. I wanted a "fair" settlement: assets, debts, and custody split straight down the middle. She wanted blood.

Even before I was arrested, Lea's salvoes in our custody battle for Logan were relentless. Once I was indicted, she didn't need to fabricate wild allegations against me anymore. The indictment gave her all the ammunition she needed. The indictment seemed to legitimize all of the other wild and baseless accusations she made in the past.

My ability to fight back—to make rational and calm rebuttals each time Lea unloaded the artillery in my direction—was weakened by the indictment. The scent of a potential felony was rank enough to give Lea some purchase to her claims. My actual concerns about Lea, supported by her own admissions to the court about her recreational drug use and sojourns into the adult industry, landed on deaf ears.

As a father who owned guns the court looked at me as a danger to my son. Amplified by the allegations of my ex-wife, the family court judge ordered me to undergo a mental health evaluation to make sure it was "safe" for my son to spend time with me.

I saw a therapist in South Jersey, and spent an hour talking to him about the divorce, work, and what I wanted as a father. He was familiar with my family and had counseled my brother through his rough patches. If anything, I was worried he might have a bias against me—after all, I had no idea what my brother had said about me or anyone else in my family after years of therapy—but he was unbiased and objective. He sent the court a letter stating that, while the divorce "seemed acrimonious" he couldn't see "any reason" why I shouldn't be able to see my son as often as possible.

Unsatisfied, Lea's attorney demanded I see a psychiatrist of his choosing, and demanded the evaluation be done at my expense. The judge, as was becoming common, acquiesced to his ultimatum. A week later I met with an "approved" psychiatrist who worked in an office conveniently located several hours from where I lived. His findings were the same as the first.

But that wasn't good enough. Lea's attorney insisted on yet another mental health evaluation—it seemed he would just keep trying until someone found something wrong with me or until I ran out of money to oblige his clients demands— and the result was the same as always.

I'd undergone four mental health evaluations by therapists, psychologists, and psychiatrists and they all said the same thing: "I see no reason why he shouldn't be able to have unsupervised visitation with his son."

The judge finally seemed to be catching on to their games, and I petitioned the court to allow me to see my son. In that petition, I also requested that the court provide me with additional visitation to make up for all of the occasions Lea had violated the Parenting Time Order. To my surprise, the judge agreed. After an eternity battling in the courts to see my son I was finally able to spend time with him unsupervised. The days of supervised visitations confined to a windowless backroom in the Ocean County Public Library were over. The judge agreed that Lea had been violating my parental rights and fined her $500. More importantly, he awarded me compensatory time to make up for all of the times Lea had kept Logan from me. My relationship with my son was finally on the upswing, and I had done it all without a lawyer.

Our bitter fight over Logan lasted longer than our marriage, which didn't even cross the six-month threshold.

Lea and I had met before a party at Rutgers the summer between my junior and senior years, introduced by a mutual friend, the rare kind of guy who breezed through Calc 5 exams in the morning and funneled 40's by early afternoon. Ducky, as he was known, was everyone's friend and if he was friends with her, than that was good enough for me. Lea thrived in the college party scene. Like Ducky, everyone seemed to love her.

We began dating almost immediately and, while we still frequented the College Avenue house parties and spandexed 80's mixers, I began to bring her on my weekend trips to enjoy the solitude of the mountains. Lea and I climbed Mt. Washington, the tallest mountain in the Northeast, together one week and traversed the Franconia Ridge another. She had no interest in ice climbing or snowboarding, my two favorite winter activities, but she thrived in the fresh air of New Hampshire's mountains.

It wasn't long before I met Lea's family. Her parents had separated over a decade earlier, and her grown-siblings lived in their childhood home with their aging mother—a woman who disliked me from the moment we met. In those days I was about as conservative as someone could be. I was a capitalist who had a part-time job as a data researcher for a private sector intel firm and was a staunch supporter of George W. Bush and the Iraq War.

In her mother's eyes, the only thing worse than a man was a conservative man.

Lea traveled with me to Europe as part of my senior year's thesis on Altitude Physiology and Climber's Risk Assessment, paid for in part by the long hours I spent working to track Politically Exposed Persons (PEPs) and Financially Exposed Persons (FEPs) throughout the twenty-two republics of Russia for a company that provided this information through software licenses to major banks and organizations around the globe. The work ethic I picked up as a tween delivering newspapers at four o'clock in the morning had clearly paid off. Together we climbed the travertine steps of Sacré Cœur de Montmartre, ate stale baguettes at a café around the cobblestoned corner from the Louvre, toured the Rubenshuis in Antwerp and the canals and museums of Amsterdam. For a senior in college, life was pretty good.

Lea's father lived alone in an apartment in Jersey City. He owned the building, a single-family Victorian turned into eight less-than-legal apartments that he had inherited from his mother. He and I got along immediately. By the time I met him he was practically bed-ridden. We would visit to go food-shopping for him and, after helping him from his bed to the couch, he would tell me stories about all of the girls he had fallen in love with in Cuba and how he still had a guy who would smuggle cigars to him from Havana. For every story he told me I'd counter with one of my own. His favorites were my exploits in the mountains, especially how my friend and I had rope-soloed a 1,200 foot cliff in New Hampshire and the time Bob Timmer and I had been the first people to ever climb a small vertical wall of ice up in Vermont.

To say we enjoyed hanging out with each other would be an understatement.

Lea was clearly upset about her father's failing health, and the more ill he fell the angrier she became at her mother. From age eight to eighteen Lea and her siblings were told their father wanted nothing to do with them, that he didn't care about them and didn't want to see them.

That couldn't have been further from the truth.

According to Lea, her father was diagnosed with terminal cancer when her parents were still together. Something happened that the kids never knew about and their mother filed for divorce and kicked him out of the house. Lea's mother knew he didn't have much time left to live and, according to her kids, hoped he would just die and be out of their lives forever.

But he didn't die.

Her father lived another ten years, proving many of the doctors wrong. He wanted to see his children, but every time he tried Lea's mother would hide them at a friend's house.

One time, Lea told me, her mother went so far as to load all of the kids on a train to Florida just to keep her father from picking them up for the weekend. This went on for a decade before the kids were old enough to learn the truth on their own. For most of her childhood, Lea thought her father didn't love her. She hated him. When she found out the truth she turned that hatred towards her mother.

As if all of the warning signs weren't there already, Lea's father sat me down on his faded leather couch one day while she made his favorite espresso in one of those stainless steel stovetop espresso makers, all noise and steam. Lea was pregnant and he was concerned I was going to try and make an "honest woman" out of her. He was right.

"Brian," he said with a strained voice looking me in the eyes, "she's a wonderful girl now... but she was mean when she was younger, just like her mother."

Over the noise of the espresso machine he told me, for my own good, not to marry her. He had stopped believing in marriage as an institution a long time ago and I thought his words were more philosophical than cautionary. I knew Lea. She wasn't this evil person he was talking about.

"Don't do it Brian. If you ask, she'll say yes." I looked in the kitchen and watched Lea filling the cupboards with the food we had just stocked up on, wondering if an evil person could really lurk beneath the makeup and seemingly sincere smiles.

I placated him while Lea brought him his espresso. He loved her, but I could see in his eyes that he really was afraid of what she was capable of. I wondered what vile things she could have possibly said or done to him to make him feel that way. I decided it was just the ramblings of a bitter old man on his deathbed and, with Lea in the room, he quickly changed the subject.

Now I'm not so sure he was wrong.

Within months I would propose to Lea, help carry her father's casket, and walk from graduation into an entry-level corporate desk job. For a short time we lived as an engaged couple in a spare bedroom at her mother's house in Toms River. It was a difficult place to live. Not because we were living together and weren't married. Her family was used to that sort of thing. Lea's sister had a child out of wedlock with a legitimate crack head, and all of her siblings enjoyed experimenting with the full spectrum of narcotics. If anything, her home was the perfect place for an unwed couple. A liberal bastion. But Lea's mother felt like I was always judging her; that I thought I was better than she was. She hated the suit and ties I had to wear to work. She hated my father and my parents' traditional family. It was as if every time she saw me she saw the failings of her own marriage.

The round-trip commute to North Jersey every day left me exhausted, unable to give my soon-to-be-bride the attention she needed and had grown used to. It took four hours just to get to and from the office before putting in a twelve-hour workday. By the time the weekend rolled around I barely had enough time to recharge before heading back to work Monday morning. I wasn't living the life I wanted, and Lea was growing more and more irritable every week.

I needed to get out and away from the congestion and confinement of life in the Northeast. In a calculated move, I reached out to my company's competitors in Denver. I would have asked for a transfer if the company I was working for had offices out West, but they didn't. With nothing but the promise of an interview, I handed in my resignation and Lea and I drove out West to Colorado.

We moved into a studio apartment in Boulder with a gorgeous patio view of the Flatirons and, within a week, I had the job.

The hours were better, the commute was better, and we were within striking distance of a half dozen parks where we could get fresh air and enjoy each others company before I had to dive back into work on Monday mornings and start the cycle all over again. We spent weekends hiking together at the Garden of the Gods and in Estes Park, but Lea still wasn't happy. She felt entitled to more. She hated the apartment and wanted nicer things, especially a house. I tried to tell her that we just needed to struggle for a little while and save up as much as we could before taking on a mortgage. I had only been out of college for a few months, and I wanted to build a financial safety net before doing anything drastic, but Lea was adamant: she had to have a house, or else.

Part of what I thought was her craziness, I'm sure, was just the needs of a nesting newlywed and mother-to-be. The rest was the leftover entitlement mentality of a youngest daughter who had grown accustomed to batting her eyes and having her dying father break out the checkbook. We pooled what resources we had, including generous gifts from my parents and her father's estate, and bought the only decent house on the market in our price range: a three bedroom house that was recently foreclosed on in the burbs between Boulder and Denver. Just two months after eloping to Rocky Mountain National Park, where we were married on the grassy shore of a lake surrounded by mountains, we moved into our new home.

The new house required lots of work, but with the coming arrival of our son we made sure it had everything it needed to be a home. Like most soon-to-be parents we spent fewer weekends hiking in the mountains, and more of our free time browsing the aisles of Babies-R-Us, picking out toys, diapers, clothes, and bottles. One day, I got a phone call at the office that Lea had gone into labor. I made it to the hospital with time to spare, and our son was born beneath Boulder's iconic Flatirons on the 15th of February.

We named him Logan, a concession Lea granted to me as a nod to my Scottish heritage. But I also liked what the name meant. I believe words have meanings, as do names, and that people tend to live up to the name they are given. Logan is the name of a charismatic leader who often undertakes large endeavors with great success. They value truth, justice, and discipline, and are quick-tempered with those who do not share those same values. The name seemed worthy of my son—and worthy of living up to.

To this day becoming a father is one of the greatest, and most magical, experiences of my life. I looked forward to his birth with excitement and trepidation. Every day I thought about all of the things we'd be able to do together and all of the experiences we would share. Lea glowed with excitement. She had wanted to be a mother since she was a teenager, years before I met her, and now she finally was. The moment Logan was born, he grabbed my finger with his tiny hand and I knew everything was going to be ok. I felt an overwhelming wave of emotion looking into his eyes, and I finally knew what my dad meant when he used to say, "one day, when you're a father, you'll understand what I'm talking about." I understood. And I was enamored with this beautiful baby boy who shared my same blue eyes.

The celebration was short lived.

Two weeks later Lea came clean about the double life she had been living. Nothing was ever the same again. The beautiful gift of fatherhood was taken away in a web of bureaucratic red tape at the behest of a mother who knew her newborn son was her only weapon in a hostile divorce. That was, at least, until I won that motion for unsupervised custody and was finally able to spend real time alone with my son out of sight of the prying eyes of the court.

Despite all of her efforts to make me look like a disinterested and dead-beat father—she even tried convincing the judge that I never even showed up for Logan's birth—I had finally won. Logan and I spent our first weekend hanging out at my friend's parents' house. He was already a year old and none of my friends had ever even met him. As I headed towards Bill's house with Logan tucked snugly into his car seat, I had an ominous thought that this might be the only opportunity I would have to introduce my friends to my son.

Unfortunately, I was right.

Within days of winning that monumental motion I was served with an Emergent Order to Show Cause. Lea declared that my felony indictment provided an emergency situation that warranted revoking my unsupervised parental rights altogether. She alleged that guns were evil and so I must be evil too and, therefore, kept away from our son at all costs. She pretended like we didn't buy the guns together.

The motion was heard that very same week. I argued that the charges against me were non-violent and victimless. I argued that I hadn't been found guilty of anything—only charged—and expected to be acquitted at trial once a jury heard the facts. I even argued that if they were concerned I had guns they shouldn't be, because my firearms were being held as evidence by the Mount Laurel Police Department.

Lea's lawyer just kept repeating the word "guns."

In the end Lea's fear mongering trumped my common sense. The judge decided that just because I didn't have guns now didn't mean I couldn't get guns if I wanted to—as if simply owning firearms was enough reason to remove a child from their parents. The judge withdrew my unsupervised visitation and placed onerous restrictions on when, where, and how I could see my son: Only in a room at the courthouse. Only under supervision of a police officer. But rooms were never available at the courthouse or, if a room was available, a police officer wasn't. I never saw my son again.

Rapists and murderers had an easier time seeing their children. But, in their eyes I was worse than either of those: I was a conservative.

CHAPTER FOUR

The defendant's very existence becomes a race against time. A desperate fight for survival to avoid a lifeless existence within cinderblock walls. The defendant wants to be free. Out of desperation, some will confess to crimes they didn't commit and beg leniency from the court. A desperate defendant will accept a plea deal just to end the nightmare that is fighting the State. And, in doing so, the defendant saves himself time, energy, and money. But not their soul. A substantial piece of their soul—their integrity—bleeds out when they beg mercy for a crime they did not commit.

And the machine grows stronger.

I was completely out of money, bled dry from the divorce and custody battle, without a penny to hire a lawyer to defend me against the criminal charges levied against me by the great State of New Jersey.

Somewhere, someone desperately wanted me to be found guilty. Somewhere, someone thought that owning guns was worthy of prosecution—and not a fine or a slap on the wrist, but five to ten years in prison—and I couldn't figure out why. What good would it do to incarcerate me? I didn't understand the bigger political landscape or that I had unwittingly become a pawn in a political maneuver to demonize guns and intimidate law-abiding gun owners. At the naïve age of twenty-four, I thought that all I had to do was follow the letter of the law and I would be fine. I had no idea that people like Michael Bloomberg, Harry Reid, and Nancy Pelosi had been working for years to turn gun owners into criminals. After all, I was only 11 years old when Diane Feinstein—a Democratic senator from California who owned firearms and even had a concealed carry permit—complained, after helping to pass the Assault Weapons Ban of 1993, "If I could have banned them all... I would have!" And I certainly had no idea that just months before my arrest the New Jersey Attorney General, Anne Milgram, had issued a directive to prosecute gun owners "vigorously," "strictly," and "uniformly."

The craziest part about all of this is that I didn't even consider myself a "gun" person. I only went shooting once or twice a year—just enough to shake the cobwebs off. I wasn't even a member of the NRA. Sure, I'd grown up with the same level of interest in firearms that any red-blooded

American male has, but my interest didn't go much further than the occasional trip to the shooting range to bond with my dad. To target me as the poster child for gun control seemed far-fetched and disingenuous, but the State didn't discriminate. As Milgram directed, all gun-owners were to be prosecuted "uniformly." The casual law-abiding gun owner was to be treated the same as a gang member who had just murdered an innocent person execution style—double tap to the back of the head—with a stolen gun. In the eyes of the State we were one and the same. It didn't make any sense.

I found myself penniless battling one of the largest legal machines in the country, fighting policies and legislation that had been backed by people much more influential than I could ever be. I turned to the people I had always turned to when I needed help: my parents. I knew the well was dry but I asked anyway. There were things they could do if they really didn't have the extra money. More than a month passed after my arrest and my father reached out to a lawyer he occasionally did business with: he could take on my case for a starting retainer of $20,000. Twenty. Thousand. Dollars. And that was his friends-and-family discount. I had no idea how average people defended themselves from the indiscriminate overreach of the State. I considered myself average, from a middle-class family, and I sure didn't have twenty-grand sitting around.

I drove back home to Hoboken after my consultation with my dad's lawyer and sat on the couch for an hour before

Mike came home. I still couldn't wrap my head around how much money this was going to cost me. There was no way I could come up with that kind of cash. Over our weekly feast of chicken wings and beer I told him how the meeting went. Mike was finally studying for the LSAT's and tried listening as both a prospective law-student and my oldest friend. My dad's lawyer told me I needed to have the charges dismissed before I was officially indicted by a grand jury. "Once you're indicted," the lawyer said, "it's too late."

Apparently, as it was explained to me and I explained to Mike, once an indictment is officially on the board the prosecutor can either win or lose that case. A prosecutor can "win" a case any number of ways: if the defendant pleads guilty, the prosecution wins. If the defendant accepts a plea deal, the prosecution wins. If the defendant goes to trial and a jury finds him guilty, the prosecution wins. Prosecutors with higher conviction-rates are perceived as "better" prosecutors, regardless of whether or not the people being prosecuted are actually guilty. Bonuses, and even careers, can depend on having high conviction rates and maintaining a perception of being "tough on crime."

In America's adversarial court system there exists a primal incentive for prosecutors not to find a just solution, but to get a conviction no matter what. I needed a lawyer to get the charges thrown out—and it needed to happen fast.

There wasn't much Mike could do to help. He'd recently

been laid off from a major Wall Street institution and was trying to figure out what his next move was going to be. If he had twenty-grand to loan me I'm sure he would have. But he was there to do what best friends do best: he listened and cracked open another Yuengling.

Time seemed to move at odd intervals during that period of my life. Some moments dragged on forever; others were over before I could even appreciate them. Surfing the waves of North Beach ended before I even zipped up my wetsuit, but the minutes spent lying awake in bed lasted an eternity. After what could have been a few days or a few weeks, Mike approached me. He had talked to his mom about my impending indictment. In her trademark style, Mike's mom came to the rescue when all other options had been exhausted. Mike's mom had gone to high school with a guy who was now a well-respected lawyer in South Jersey, and he was able to help persuade a colleague of his to take on my case at a significantly reduced rate; practically a tenth of what my dad's lawyer was asking.

Richard Josselson was relatively well known out of his Haddonfield office. He'd been practicing personal injury law for thirty years and had defended—unsuccessfully—the first homicide case in Camden facing the death penalty after New Jersey reinstated capital punishment in 1982. He seemed to have a great resume when it came to suing major corporations and divorcing wealthy spouses. The only problem was that, like those municipal cops who arrested me, he didn't have a clue when it came to New Jersey gun laws.

"Are you a lawyer?" Josselson asked condescendingly from his highback leather chair. His ego seemed to still be riding the wave of his lone appearance on the Montel Williams Show practically a decade earlier.

"Well, no," I replied, "but these are the laws the New Jersey State Troopers told me I had to follow when I was moving," I handed Josselson print outs of the State Police website, listing the various statutes that protected my right to transport my firearms, without a permit, from one house to another.

"You don't know what you're talking about," he said tossing the statutes aside without even looking at them. "Guns are illegal in New Jersey. You can't have them without a permit. Did you have a permit?" He stared at me for a moment, "No? Then you can't have guns in New Jersey. I don't know how they do it in Colorado, but that's how we do it here. Have you been indicted yet?"

"No. No, I don't think so."

"OK, good. We should try and get this cleaned up before you're indicted. Maybe get you probation or something, see if we can work out a deal. But that's got to happen before you're indicted. Mitnick said you were a friend of a friend, do you have money?"

"No," Josselson sat back in his chair with a look on his face that read 'Well, then what the fuck are you doing in my office?'

"But my friend's mom agreed to help me out."

"Ok," he leaned forward, "it's gonna be thirty-five hundred bucks and I need it before I do anything. Is that going to be a problem?"

With Josselson retained I felt like I finally had a chance, but he kept talking about "making a deal" of some kind or another. I didn't want to make a deal. There were no deals to be made. I hadn't broken any laws and I hadn't hurt a single person. The State couldn't name a victim if they tried. So, why would I confess to something I didn't do, even if it meant a reduced sentence?

Josselson placated my idealism and I really believe he thought I'd change my mind. That the overwhelming weight of facing ten years in prison would simply compel me to sellout and take the first merciful offer that came my way.

But I had no intention of making a deal with the State. Ever.

Unknown to me or Josselson at the time, the State had already convened a grand jury to investigate whether or not I should formally face charges. The role of a grand jury is to sift through the evidence provided by the state to determine whether or not a charge should move forward toward trial.

Led by the Burlington County Prosecutor, Robert Bernardi, the grand jury was told I had guns, hollow-point bullets, and "high-capacity" magazines: scary words used to describe common things lots of gun owners have in their house. Conveniently, Bernardi left out all of the statutes that specifically exempted me from what I was charged with.

Bernardi had no problem getting the indictment.

As New York State chief judge Sol Wachtler famously told Tom Wolfe "a grand jury would 'indict a ham sandwich,' if that's what you wanted." A New Jersey grand jury, apparently, wasn't much different.

The cogs of the machine were moving, and there was no chance of having the case dismissed without a fight. With the indictment official, the prosecutor was under pressure to ensure a guilty verdict. Even Chris Christie, the Governor of New Jersey, ran for office on the fact that he was "tough on crime," with a solid conviction rate as a federal prosecutor.

To Christie's credit, he earned his reputation winning convictions, or receiving guilty pleas, from over 130 corrupt public officials without losing a single case—not the least of which included the prosecution of State Senator and Newark mayor Sharpe James for mail fraud, wire fraud, and conspiring to rig the sale of nine city lots to his mistress. Even the historically liberal *New York Times* praised the Republican prosecutor as winning "widespread admiration for his aggressive fight against political corruption."

A prosecutor's conviction rate can make or break a career and, when Assistant Prosecutor John Brennan was assigned the task of convicting me I believe he had every intention of doing so, and he wasn't going to let a little thing like the truth get in his way.

In Josselson's first act as my attorney, he filed a well thought out motion to have all of the physical evidence obtained by the police officers made inadmissible in court. If the Motion to Dismiss was successful, none of the evidence—the guns, ammunition, or magazines—would be allowed to be considered by the judge or jury at trial. Without the evidence, there was no case. Without the evidence, there was no trial.

In his brief to the court, Josselson argued that my Fourth Amendment rights were violated—that when Officer Joy called me a second time, he coerced me to come back under the threat of arrest and, later, coerced me into signing the consent form to search my car or face being committed to a psychiatric hospital. It was Josselson's position that the entire stop—if it could even be considered a stop—was a flagrant violation of my most basic and fundamental constitutional rights.

In legal circles this is known as the "fruit of the poisonous tree" argument; a metaphor used to describe evidence that is obtained illegally. If the source (the "tree") of the evidence is tainted, then anything gained (the "fruit") from it is tainted as well.

Josselson also argued that the evidence resulted from a two and a half hour interrogation, before or during which I was never read my Miranda warning.

Oral arguments for the motion were heard on June 22, 2009 just weeks after the family court judge revoked custody of my son. The motion was heard in a courtroom on the 6th floor of the Burlington County Superior Court in Mount Holly.

Officer Joy did not look happy about being cross examined by my lawyer.

"Would it be fair to say," Josselson opened, "that when you put out an all-points-bulletin, it was not only as you put it, to Mount Laurel police officers, but other surrounding jurisdictions, that if they saw this license plate that you had, they ought to stop and pickup Mr. Aitken?"

Officer Joy adjusted his blue shirt, looked at me, and gave his rehearsed one word answer: "Yes."

"Okay," Josselson went on, "and were they then to return Mr. Aitken to the Mount Laurel Police Department?"

"Preferably, or the scene, or just have him come back."

"Okay. Bring him back?"

"Yes."

"All right. Would it be fair to state that you had two conversations with Mr. Aitken, the first one, you spoke with Mr. Aitken and he said to you "I'm not suicidal, I don't have any guns, I'm on my way to move up to North Jersey and I don't want to come back." And that was the end of the discussion. And, within a few seconds, maybe a minute, you called him back and basically told him, "Get back here. If you don't they're gonna pick you up.""

Josselson was trying to establish that I was coerced into coming back—under threat of arrest—without probable cause and, so far, Joy was giving us everything we needed.

"Yes," Joy said defensively, staring at me again before looking back at Josselson, "but we didn't make any threats to him or anything like that."

"Hold on a second," Judge Morley interrupted, "Did you tell him that if he didn't come back and was located by the police, he would be brought back to either the station or the location?"

I couldn't tell if the judge was trying to get to the truth or if he was trying to help Officer Joy back out of admitting he'd clearly shit all over my constitutional rights. Joy looked like a deer about to get clobbered by an eighteen-wheeler. He didn't know which answer to give: the truth, or the one that would keep him out of trouble.

"I can't remember."

"Okay," Josselson looked up at the judge for permission to continue with his cross-examination. Morley waved him on, "Now, would it be a fair statement to say that when Mr. Aitken came back from his parents' home, he wasn't free to leave, correct?"

"During the investigation, we wanted to ask more questions. He wasn't under arrest or anything."

"Did you hear me ask you that?" my lawyer shot back.

We were getting everything we needed on the record, but my lawyers little outbursts were starting to worry me. I could tell he was getting fed up with the police officer's practiced one-word answers and selective memory. Josselson seemed determined to pull the truth out of Joy one word at a time.

"Hold on, hold on," the judge interrupted again, "If Mr. Aitken, at that point, had turned around and walked to his car, towards his car, what would you have done?"

"I probably would've gotten between him and his car and said 'You're not free to leave until we're through with the matter."

"Thank you, Judge. I think that made it clear. He wasn't free to leave, correct?"

"No."

I suddenly felt a massive weight lift off my shoulders—as if the truth might actually stand a chance. Joy had testified that, within the meaning of the law, I was detained. Josselson explained to me that, according to a landmark Fourth Amendment case known as *State v Brown,* there are four factors to determine if a person is in custody:

1. Duration of custody;
2. Nature and degree of pressure applied to detain the individual;
3. Physical surroundings of the questioning, and;
4. The language used in summoning the individual.

I had been held for the better part of three hours; was told that all of the police in New Jersey were out looking for me and that they were to "stop and hold" me if they found me; was forced to sit on the ground with a police officer standing guard over me, and; Officer Joy even testified that if I tried to leave he would "stop me" and tell me I "was not free to leave."

Without evidence of criminal activity, Josselson had explained to me, it is illegal for an officer to hold someone against their will. Not to mention that once someone is not free to leave, anything they say or do can be used against them and I was never read my Miranda Warning—the one that tells you to shut up and get a lawyer—until hours later, after I had already answered the police officers questions for almost three hours. Officer Joy's memory—not surprisingly

—was different. Joy claimed he read me my Miranda Warning, but just didn't have me sign the card acknowledging my right to remain silent until several hours later at the police department, after I'd already been interrogated.

"All right," Josselson continued, "So he's there and he's not free to leave. You started questioning him, correct?"

"Yes."

"Okay. You had never given him his Miranda Warnings at that point in time, correct?"

"No." Joy seemed to be sticking to one-word answers.

"Okay, and just so I have it correct, you asked him permission to search his vehicle, he gives it to you, you read him the consent form, tell him to look it over, and he signs it right there?"

"Yes."

"And your testimony is, shortly after you found the guns and ammunition in the trunk, you read him the Miranda Warnings."

"Yes."

"But, unlike the consent form, you didn't have him sign the Miranda card right then and there?"

Joy testified that he didn't keep Miranda cards in his car, which he needs for each and every arrest he makes. He testified that he only kept the more rarely used consent forms—the document someone signs giving the police permission to search their car.

Joy seemed like a good soldier—the kind of guy you'd want under your command because he'd do what he was told without question. On the stand, Joy appeared more concerned with the potential repercussions he might face from his superiors for testifying "incorrectly" instead of embracing the fact that, if he told the truth, he might save an innocent man from spending up to ten years in prison. His professional self-preservation was more important than my life.

"So, in other words, if—whatever the situation is, wherever a stop could be—you place someone under arrest and you give them the Miranda Warnings, it could be a matter of hours before they actually sign them, that's what you're testifying to?"

"Yes."

Joy was, as *The Washington Post* calls it, 'testilying'. Police officers lying on the stand has been a problem for as far back as the occupation goes. But, no one wants to believe that a cop would lie. We trust them implicitly and they risk their lives to keep us safe. They would never lie. But they do. And they always have. Fifty years ago, former U.S. attorney and New York criminal judge Irving Younger wrote for *The Nation* that:

> Every lawyer who practices in the criminal courts knows that police perjury is commonplace. The reason is not hard to find. Policemen see [themselves] as fighting a two-front war—against criminals in the street and against "liberal" rules of law in court. All's fair in this war, including the use of perjury to subvert "liberal" rules of law that might free those who "ought" to be jailed. And even if his lies are exposed in the courtroom, the policeman is as likely to be indicted for perjury by his co-worker, the prosecutor, as he is to be struck down by thunderbolts from an avenging heaven.

Testilying is just as common today—if not more so—than it was when Younger wrote those words in 1967.

"Okay," Josselson said continuing his cross of Officer Joy, "his mother never told you that she believed he had firearms on him, did she?"

"She said that she knew he had firearms, but didn't know if he had them with him at the time."

"Right. So, when you put the call out and when he came back, you had no indication at all that he had guns, correct?"

"It was unknown."

"He didn't commit any kind of crime, correct?"

"Not that I know of."

Not that he knew of. The correct answer was: no. I was never a suspect in a crime and none of the police officers thought I was going to commit a crime. But they demanded I return to Mount Laurel or get "picked up" by police who were apparently out looking for me, without any probable cause, whatsoever. The New Jersey Supreme Court, in *New Jersey v Carty*, has upheld a need for probable cause to exist before police officers can even ask permission to search a car. In the Court's 2002 decision, Judge Sylvia Pressler—a fellow Rutgers alumnus—wrote:

> In order for a consent to search a motor vehicle and its occupants to be valid, law enforcement personnel must have a reasonable and articulable suspicion of criminal wrongdoing prior to seeking consent to search a lawfully stopped motor vehicle.

The only way around requiring probable cause to search a car in New Jersey is by establishing exigent circumstances through the 'Community Caretaking Doctrine.' This code allows for police officers to subvert the probable cause requirement if it is in the best interest of community safety. If, for example, the police officers legitimately believed I was suicidal they would be allowed to search my car without needing to establish any probable cause of criminal wrongdoing.

Josselson went in for the kill.

"You never called a Crisis Center, you never took him to a hospital, you never did anything of that nature, did you?"

"No." Joy said defiantly, as if to really ask 'Who the fuck do you think you are?'

"When you thought he was suicidal and you got him on the cell phone and he was on his way back, you didn't have an ambulance waiting there for him and you didn't take him right to a Crisis Center, did you?"

"Well, that's up to the officer's discretion."

"You're the officer?"

"Yes."

"Right. And I'm saying, you didn't do it?"

"Yes."

"In your discretion, you didn't think it was necessary?"

"No."

"Judge, that's all I have for now."

Joy had testified over and over that he didn't think I was actually suicidal. The truth, as best as I have been able to decipher it over the past several years, is that my mom told Officer Joy I owned guns and he wanted to find them. That was it. It was a gun hunt from the very beginning, nothing more.

With the testimony on the record that Officer Joy had ordered me to come back under threat of arrest, searched my car without probable cause, interrogated me for hours without Mirandizing me—topped off with the fact that he never actually believed I was suicidal—I was sure we were going to win the motion to suppress the evidence.

But in Josselson's closing argument I began to realize just how much power the badge held—even with Officer Joy's own sworn testimony working against him.

"Do you ask me to disbelieve the officer?" the judge asked my lawyer, "You want me to find that the officer just lied to me?"

"Yes," Josselson said, defeated, "which I know the court won't."

Both the judge and the prosecutor conceded that Officer Joy had no probable cause to search my car and the judge went on to ignore Officer Joy's sworn testimony that he didn't believe I was suicidal so that he could uphold the search as being lawful under the Community Caretaking Doctrine— even though the officer's own testimony conflicted with the judge's conclusion.

The motion was denied: all of the evidence, no matter how it was obtained, would be admissible in trial.

In an effort to avoid the time-consuming process of trial, the State offered me one plea deal after another. The plea deal was always the same: a five-year sentence with a one-year minimum mandatory before I'd be eligible for parole.

The judge seemed to think it was a great deal.

"Mr. Aitken," he said to me one day, "you had guns in New Jersey. That's against the law. You're guilty and you're going to go to jail. Take the plea deal—it's only a year. You're a young man. You'll spend a year in prison, get out, and bounce right back."

I doubt he would have felt the same way if his son were in my shoes.

Plea deals are commonly offered to avoid the costly process of going to trial—for both the State and the defendant. With practically all pleas, the defendant admits culpability, if not outright guilt, but avoids trial and usually gets a softer sentence.

> "During an arraignment the defendant is faced with the maximum charge or punishment that the defendant will be held to if he or she goes to trial. The prosecutor will present the defendant with an opportunity to plead guilty to a lesser charge or to the original charge with less than the maximum sentence" – Bureau of Justice Assistance

In the best of cases, this is used to keep the trial calendar from jamming up with cases where the defendant is clearly guilty and is willing to waive their right to trial. Sometimes, plea offers are used as a way to compel innocent people to "take a deal" so all parties can avoid the significant expenses and risks associated with going to trial.

According to the Federal Justice Statistics, in 2009, less than five percent of defendants in criminal cases actually exercised their right to speedy, public trial with an impartial jury—as guaranteed by the 6th Amendment.

In a 2012 academic study that attempted to recreate why and how an innocent person might plead guilty, students at the Florida Institute of Technology were told they had been caught cheating on a logic test as part of a psychological study. If the students confessed to cheating and saved the university the time and money of going to trial in front of the Academic Review Board, they would only lose their right to compensation for participating in the study. However, if they maintained their innocence and proceeded to trial—and were found guilty—they would lose the compensation, their faculty adviser would be informed, and they would be forced to enroll in an ethics course. The students had no idea this was the real study.

Fifty-six percent of the innocent students chose to admit culpability rather than risk going before the review board.

Just like in real life, the defendants would be "rewarded" for accepting a plea deal and—if found guilty—punished for exercising their right to trial. I'm not anti-plea-deals under the right circumstances and for the right people, but clearly the prosecutor really wanted to avoid taking my case to trial.

I turned the offer down, just as I had done every other time before.

I'd lost everything by this point. The State had taken my son and now they were gunning for me. With nothing left to lose, I chose to stand and fight. If nothing else, I could set an example for the son they wouldn't let me be a father to. I could show him that the men in our family don't back down from what is right, and we don't cower to men in robes or men with guns. I'd rather let a jury see the facts and decide my fate than confess to a crime I didn't commit.

I vowed then and there to take this as far as was necessary.

Josselson wasn't happy. He was sick of representing a guy who wouldn't just take a plea deal like everyone else. He finally told me one day that if I was going to refuse to make a deal with the State than he would need more money, a few thousand dollars, to continue to represent me.

I reminded him—as politely as a desperate man can—that he agreed to represent me for a fixed amount until trial, and that we had a long road to go before we even got there. When I told him I didn't have any more money to give him —and that I felt like he was trying to extort me because this case was turning out to be more than he had bargained for

—he filed for a Motion to be Relieved as Counsel.

Technically, a lawyer can't drop a client because of their inability to pay—especially if they've already paid in full—so Josselson told the court he needed to stop being my lawyer because we didn't get along anymore. The truth was that Josselson hadn't anticipated my resolve. He thought I would take a plea deal and he would cash my friends check and call it a day. When he realized I was serious about taking this to trial, he wanted out—and felt entitled to all of the money I had paid him.

The judge had no problem obliging him and, a year off from trial, I was facing the State alone—again.

CHAPTER FIVE

Sometimes the best things in life happen when you least expect them.

I first met Jenna's parents at a house party in upstate New York, ninety miles north of the city. A few months earlier I had moved from Hoboken; sick of living in New Jersey and desperately searching for a place where I could just spread out, breathe, and enjoy life again. City life had become claustrophobic and empty all at the same time. Few places are as lonely as a big city. I've always thought you can only really get to know someone if you spend time with them in the mountains.

My house was a small-whitewashed studio on a wooded six-acre lot on the outskirts of an old hamlet called High Falls. I had filed the Articles of Incorporation to start my own digital publishing company, rescued a dog I named Frankenstein from the local no-kill shelter, and started down the bootstrapped road of entrepreneurship—spending up to eighty hours a week coding and 'dialing for dollars' to setup meetings with anyone I thought might be able to help me get this company off the ground. At four-hundred bucks a month, my small cabin was the best deal around. Sure, there was a catch: I had to mow the lawn for the eighty-eight year old landowner and drive him to and from his dialysis appointments three times a week. But Ronka was an awesome guy to hang out with. I never got tired of his stories about traveling the world before television even existed.

Time slowed down and chaos was replaced with sundrenched daily barbeques and new friends—most of who came to this small village in search of the same peace and tranquility I'd found there.

The party where I met Jenna's parents was down the hill at my neighbors' house. It was one of those hot summer nights that made the beer taste better and the stars shine brighter. My neighbor had been telling me for months that I needed to meet her niece, a writer in the city with nomadic tendencies, but the opportunity never presented itself. At that very moment Jenna was halfway through a cross-country road trip camping somewhere on the California coast—which was quite the feat, considering she'd never driven a car a day in her life. Barbie and Neil were out on the deck overlooking the cliffs when my neighbor introduced us under the glowing orbs of the Chinese lanterns.

We spent the night trading stories under the moonlight. I told them how I'd left my publishing job in the city and was striking out on my own and, naturally, left out that I'd been recently indicted—although that was probably the most interesting thing about me at the time. They finished each others sentences telling me about how they'd met in Greece while Barbie was traveling abroad, how they'd married in secret, and how Neil—a Brit from the London suburbs—smuggled himself into the States through the Canadian border in the trunk of a car so he could spend the rest of his life with Barbara. It wasn't long before they both brought up their youngest daughter, Jenna, who I "absolutely HAD to meet."

I could hear the distinctive boom of my other neighbor, Aidan Quinn—the actor known almost exclusively to me as the guy who played the eldest brother alongside Brad Pitt in Legends of the Fall, coming from all the way across the house when Barbie broke out her cell phone to call Jenna. "He's so dynamic!" I could hear her saying as I walked away, "you HAVE to meet him! And his eyes are SO blue!"

That was just the way High Falls was back then. In the morning you could be drenched in the summer sun climbing some of the best quartzite conglomerate in the country, and by nightfall someone would follow the music to the tiki torches and you'd have new friends. Sometimes those people were fellow travelers—many of them broke and embarking on some spiritual journey or another—other times they were locals, farmers or teachers, and even the occasional actor of both the struggling and Hollywood variety. It was rumored Steve Buscemi had a house up the road, but he never stumbled into any of my backyard parties to play horseshoes with us. It was a strange and magical place to live.

Days and weeks passed, but eventually Jenna returned from her bohemian roadtrip and we met for coffee at my favorite cafe in New Paltz. Within no time, we were spending every waking moment with each other. Her company provided a welcome distraction from the chaos that had become my life, and she brought a much needed feminine touch to smooth out the rough edges of my relatively newfound—but warmly embraced—bachelorhood.

Those saltwater days of summer were punctuated with the growing concern that my trial date was inching closer, and I had no lawyer to help me navigate the grey waters of what passed for justice in New Jersey. My desperate desire to stay out of prison eventually trumped my need for privacy and I made the difficult decision to go public with my case.

I had no idea how people would react.

In early August of 2009 I was invited to tell my story to Judge Andrew Napolitano—a former life appointed judge in New Jersey—on his show 'Freedomwatch' from his studio several stories above 6th Avenue in the FOX News headquarters.

Nervous, but determined, I walked through the familiar streets of Manhattan up to the imposing entrance of 1211 Avenue of the Americas—home base for Rupert Murdoch's conservative media empire. Going public with my story was a big gamble. I didn't know if I could trust the media to tell my story accurately, but I knew, after Josselson dumped me and left me without any legal representation, that I had no other choice but to appeal to the public for help.

Between guests, a producer introduced me to Napolitano. While I shook hands with the Judge—who was much shorter than I anticipated—a very tan looking fellow from Kentucky was sitting on stage waiting to announce his U.S. Senate bid. Seated across from me in the greenroom, another well-sunned gentleman from Connecticut was prepping his talking points about how he saw the real-estate crash coming before anyone else. I had never heard of either of these two before in my life, and I most certainly did not get the spray-tan memo.

I didn't belong there. I wasn't involved in politics or economics. I was just a kid who knew what was right and who wasn't going to let some small-town cops and a judge who didn't like my values put me behind bars. Not without a fight, anyway. I belonged back home in the mountains with my son, but the detour to get there cut right through downtown Manhattan and past the eight-foot tall blonde women of FOX News. Things were getting weird.

On stage, the lights were blinding and I heard Judge Napolitano shouting, "I am happy to meet you because you are a lover of freedom, and a defender of freedom, although your rights in the Garden State have not been upheld by the judicial system." Napolitano is the exception to the rule, holding the distinction of not only always being the loudest person in the room, but often also the most logical.

The Judge—as everyone on set referred to him—spent his career as a lawyer, superior court judge, and professor of constitutional law at Seton Hall University. It was difficult to imagine anyone who could know New Jersey's laws better than him.

"Jersey is not a gun-friendly state," the Judge boomed into the camera, "I can tell you as a former life-tenured judge in that state, it is not a friend of the Second Amendment."

The segment was over.

I was quickly shuffled offstage and, with my fifteen minutes of fame over, I headed back out into the summer streets of New York. I wondered if anyone would care. If my appearance on the show would make any difference at all. I was convinced people had enough problems of their own, without dropping everything to help out a complete stranger. I got through those days reminding myself that worse things have happened to better people, and I had earned quite the stiff upper lip by then. I walked anonymously through the city to Grand Central, boarded a northbound train, and fell asleep thinking about what my son might be up to and what he might think of his father one day—when he was old enough to see the truth.

Even in my sleep, all I could think about was the court's apathy towards me so far. I didn't expect anything would change. The court didn't seem to give a shit about me, so why should anyone else?

I couldn't have been more wrong.

The next morning I woke up to hundreds of emails and Facebook messages from people who had seen the show. They all said the same thing:

"Brian, I saw you on Freedomwatch. I can't believe what's happening to you. What can we do to help?"

In my eagerness and desperation to share my story, I had completely overlooked any sort of call to action. People wanted to help but didn't know how and I hadn't thought that far ahead. I didn't expect people to actually care.

Strangers were quick to offer words of support and advice. Dozens of people told me I needed to hire an attorney— which I thought was kind of a no-brainer at that point. The strange thing was that everyone was recommending I hire the same lawyer, a guy named Evan Nappen. I quickly looked him up online, and was not impressed with his website that looked like it had been built in the frontier days of AOL and MySpace. His goatee and ponytail weren't exactly confidence inspiring, either.

A deeper dive into his background showed Nappen had written a number of books specifically about New Jersey gun laws—and had a pretty kick-ass track record forcing liberal judges and police chiefs to acknowledge that pesky little piece of paper otherwise known as the Bill of Rights.

If nothing else, my appearance on 'Freedomwatch' helped my mom and dad understand just how dire the situation had become and, with a loan from my parents, I hired Nappen sight unseen—based on his reputation, alone.

+++

"Ok, Brian, there are a couple things I want to talk to you about," I heard Richard Gilbert's voice over the phone. Richard was an attorney for Evan Nappen's law firm and was assigned to my case, "We've submitted a request to the National Rifle Association's Institute for Legislative Action and they've agreed to finance your trial, so we'll be sending you a check to reimburse what you've paid us already."

"That's amazing," I didn't know what else to say. I was floored. The momentum from my appearance on Freedomwatch was picking up. People were starting to notice

—and they cared.

"Yes, and we'd like to file a Motion to Dismiss the charges. You'll be getting something in the mail but we'll need you to be in court on November 30, ok?"

Things were moving fast and anything that might get the charges dismissed sounded great to me.

"Thanks, Richard. Is there anything I can do to help?"

"Just sit tight and meet me outside the courtroom before the hearing, ok?"

"Ok."

My first call with Richard was brief—but thorough—and after the call I finally felt like I was in good hands. I just hoped this high point wasn't as short-lived as my motion for custody had been.

I can't remember much of the weeks leading up to the hearing for the motion to dismiss, except for a phone call Jenna got from her father shortly after her birthday in late October.

"Jenna," her father asked, "have you ever Googled your boyfriend?"

Welcome to dating in the twenty-first century.

Jenna and I hadn't officially even been dating for more than a few weeks, although Jenna might have viewed this differently, as sometimes happens when two people gradually move from meeting for coffee in the morning to meeting over beers in the evening. Neither of us had even started to think about when the appropriate time would be to tell her parents about my baggage. It seemed a little premature to me, since I'd only met her parents twice by that point, but I made sure Jenna knew early on what she was getting into. I told her more times than she cares to remember that I was not looking for a serious relationship. That too much had happened too recently and that I had too much to figure out on my own without taking on the responsibility of caring for —or loving—another person. But, sometimes a thing comes to exist whether or not the timing is right and, regardless of what you call it, it is what it is.

I could tell Jenna was uneasy. Her parents were upset and, more than anything, she wanted their approval—which I thought was strange, since they were the ones who had played matchmaker in the first place. They hadn't only found out about the indictment, but they had found out about the divorce and my son as well—the two practically went hand-in-hand with each other. After getting off the phone with Jenna, I sat down at my desk, looked out at the deer trail that led up and over the mountain to a farm on the other side, opened my laptop and wrote her this email:

November 2, 2009

Hi Jenna,

Just wanted to drop you a line... I know we got off the phone like 20 seconds ago, but I still feel terrible about you feeling terrible!

I feel like, because your parents are upset, that I should have some sort of defense to show them... but, honestly, I don't. The only thing I did wrong was marry a girl that I hardly knew because we were going to have a child together and we thought it was love when we were just young and naive. She is still both. Worse, she allows her emotions to dictate her life and, consequently, our sons life. Divorce brings out the absolute worst in people. I never made one false allegation against her during the entire divorce. I never once lied about who she was or said anything in an attempt to discredit her. She, unfortunately, did not take the high road too. She accused me of some of the most vile things you can imagine. Something I was unprepared for is how to defend myself against absolute fabrications. How do I prove that I'm not a terrible father/husband? I can't. And she doesn't have to support her allegations, she merely needs to make them and their atrocity is enough to make a Judge "err on the side of caution."

She is a contemptible girl and I feel guilty that my son will be raised by her but there's nothing I can do. The Court System would have me throw a hundred thousand dollars more at this problem in Motions, Appeals and miscellaneous fees (mental health evaluations - I already paid for three... they all said the same thing: no reason why I shouldn't see my son unsupervised whenever I want. But as long as she continues to make allegations I need to go out and pay $1,500 to a doctor for a new evaluation. There's a term for this, it's called Parental Alienation Syndrome, and she's damn good at it. From what she told me, so was her mother. My ex didn't know her father until the year he died of cancer... she only had 10 months with him... even though he'd been battling cancer for 10 years. Why? Her mother was a vindictive woman who put her emotions in front of what was best for her family).

The important thing to me is that, no matter what steps in my way, I don't lose sight of my personal responsibility and my goals. I try not to get caught up in the things other people say and do... since I have no control over any of that. What I do have control over are the things that I do... and I like to think that I am constantly moving forward. Constantly educating myself and progressing my ability to be successful in this world... in every sense of the word. That's all I have. Cars go away. Houses burn down. Savings get spent. Peoples opinions change. Who loves you today may very well hate you tomorrow. The only thing you take to the grave is what you've accomplished and your integrity. That is what I focus my energies on. That is who I am.

Keep your head on straight.
Brian xoxo

Jenna told me her eyes lingered on the "xoxo." We hadn't yet said "I love you" or "I love you, too."

+++

When I saw Jenna's father next, I handed over the arrest report as well as the written briefs from the previous motion. He was no stranger to the law. After smuggling his way into the country, he gained his citizenship and became a court reporter. He'd seen much worse crimes than what I'd been accused of but, I think, when it's your daughter's boyfriend the nature of the charges doesn't matter at first: an indictment is an indictment.

If I know her father as well as I think I do, he probably read every line of the transcripts twice. I could practically hear his subtle but highbrow London accent reading each line to himself. I offered to walk away from his daughter forever if he thought I was the monster the government was trying to make me out to be. But he didn't. Despite our vast political differences, we found common ground: we both wanted what was best for Jenna. She was the youngest and most sheltered of his three daughters. The eldest, Jasmine, was the rebellious one. Joy, the middle daughter, was the prodigal child. He had a hard time letting go of Jenna but he didn't want to stand in the way of what she wanted.

+++

A few weeks later, Jenna came to the pre-trial hearing to support me. I guess that's when things "got real" for her. Like most sheltered middle-class suburban girls, she had only ever seen the inside of a courtroom on fieldtrips and TV shows. I, on the other hand, was becoming increasingly and uncomfortably familiar with the inside of courtrooms. I don't think she knew what she was getting herself into and, in retrospect, it probably made for a lousy date. Who knows, maybe it was exciting to finally be the girl with the boyfriend no one approved of.

We met Richard outside the courtroom, and he pointed out a spot for Jenna to sit behind the defense table where we were headed. Goatees and cheap ties must have been part of the firm's dress code. Richard wore a black tie with red silkscreened chili peppers on it that I can still picture vividly almost five years later. My dad had always told me to wear power stripes on my ties. "Bold stripes command attention and authority," he used to say. Maybe Richard was taking Cato the Elder's advice by intentionally trying to come across as a harmless plebeian instead of the tactical genius he was rumored to be.

We took our seats as the judge entered the room.

"Go ahead, sit down. Sit down," Judge Morley passively commanded as he took his own seat at the altar of justice. "The matter before the court today is a motion to dismiss the indictment. The parties have made written submissions, which I have reviewed. Mr. Gilbert, is there anything you'd like to add?"

"Yes, thank you, Your Honor." Richard said, standing up to address the court. He went on to argue that I was protected under both the New Jersey exemptions to the firearms charges as well as the federal Firearms Owners Protection Act (FOPA), which reads in part:

> "...any person who is not otherwise prohibited by this chapter from transporting, shipping, or receiving a firearm shall be entitled to transport a firearm for any lawful purpose from any place where he may lawfully possess and carry such firearm to any other place where he may lawfully possess and carry such firearm..."

"What I neglected to include," Richard continued, "is that possession of hollow-point ammunition is not only exempted for these reasons but is also exempted under 2C: 39-3g(2) which provides that it's lawful to possess hollow-points at a target range, at a person's dwelling, premises or other land owned or possessed by him and a person may carry such from the place of purchase to the above locations. This exemption was also never presented to the grand jury for its consideration and if found applicable would directly negate Mr. Aitken's guilt."

"Did the State have any factual information that would have required it to tell the grand jury about that exemption?"

"Yes, your Honor. It looks like the State is trying to cast this as a factual issue and I don't see it that way at all. This is an issue of law and I believe what was clearly established, the officer in his report indicated no less than three times that Mr. Aitken informed him that he was in the process of moving between residences. That's the real point here, Your Honor."

The prosecutor—and even the judge—seemed interested in making my case about narrowly defining what it meant to be "moving" instead of whether or not a crime had actually been committed. They had turned my life into a game.

+++

Some people maintain, even today, that what I did was "illegal" and that—while unfortunate that I could spend up to ten years in prison—I had to "pay the price" for breaking the law. But there are thousands of laws on the books—so many that the U.S. Department of Justice gave up trying to count them all—and it's estimated the average person commits up to three felonies a day[*] in the course of going about their own business. No one would be free if everyone were held to the standard of "paying the price" for breaking arbitrary and unjust laws. As Cicero said, "The more laws,

---

[*] In 2009 Boston civil-liberties lawyer Harvey Silverglate wrote the book *Three Felonies a Day* detailing how the average citizen unwittingly commits several felonies every day, from illegally streaming television shows to illegally downloading music and even selling fresh eggs or raw milk.

the less justice."

Richard continued to plead for common sense to prevail.

"A move is not a single discrete action in practical realistic terms. With a house full of stuff and a small vehicle, several trips were necessary to complete the move. I would respectfully submit that the law does not rule out a move between two residences for whatever reason. It doesn't say that a move must be made only for certain reasons."

"What if you have three residences," Morley asked from the bench, "any time you decide to spend Saturday night in one residence you can just put your guns in your car and take them to the other residences?"

"Respectfully, Your Honor, yes."

"What if you have 21 residences—you have a house in every county in the state? Can you just bring them with you when you're going from one house to another?"

"If they're legitimate residences, Your Honor, the law does not provide a limit to say you're limited to two residences. It says when moving between residences. If somebody is fortunate enough to be able to afford more than one residence, it's perfectly legitimate to do that as long as they're carried properly."

"If he told the police I brought them from Colorado and at some point I brought them to Hoboken where I intend to live and the grand jury was told that, what's wrong with the grand jury presentation?"

"Respectfully, Your Honor, what's wrong is that they weren't presented with the law that allows a person to be able to move firearms between two residences. They were only provided with a law that says if you have a gun, it's illegal, you go to jail. That's not the be all and end all. There are exemptions under New Jersey law for possession of firearms, and the grand jury wasn't provided with them."

Judge Morley sat back in his chair looking temporarily defeated.

"Does the exemption for transportation require that the weapon be in a locked container?" Morley asked the prosecutor, leaning forward into the microphone.

Brennan stood up to answer the judge, "The exemption reads that firearms shall be carried unloaded and contained in a closed and fastened case, gun box, securely tied package or locked in a trunk of an automobile."

"So it could be in a shoe box?" he asked skeptically. "Hold on a second."

The judge abruptly ordered a recess and called Richard and the prosecutor up to the bench. I could see the judge covering the microphone but couldn't hear what was being said. The judge seemed pretty unhappy right before he called the recess—like he'd walked into an ambush—but when Richard walked back to the defense table he was the one who looked unnerved.

The exemptions were never brought up again.

Richard went on to argue my right to keep and bear arms under the Second Amendment as codified by the recent Heller decision outlawing gun-banning schemes as unconstitutional. But the Second Amendment had not yet been incorporated to the States through the Fourteenth Amendment—the McDonald case that would decide this was still months away from being heard.

"Is the prohibition on carrying a firearm outside one's home or place of business without a permit a ban on ownership?" asked the judge.

"Well, see, that's the interesting thing, Your Honor. There's a difference between keeping and bearing and the Heller decision said keeping is a fundamental individual right. The decision doesn't address bearing. Bearing as defined in that decision is to have it on the person ready to instantly defend one's self. Mr. Aitken was not bearing firearms in this case— he was only keeping them. They were with his other household possessions locked in his trunk but he was keeping them with his personal possessions during the process of this move, so I believe this falls directly under the Heller decision. Of course, the McDonald case is coming down regarding Chicago and that will address the incorporation issue."

In the landmark *Heller* decision, the U.S. Supreme Court held in a 5-4 opinion that the Second Amendment protects an individual's right to possess a firearm for traditionally lawful purposes and that the capital's ban on gun ownership was unconstitutional.

> Nowhere else in the Constitution does a 'right' attributed to 'the people' refer to anything other than an individual right. What is more, in all six other provisions of the Constitution that mention 'the people,' the term unambiguously refers to all members of the political community, not an unspecified subset... The Second Amendment extends, prima facie, to all instruments that constitute bearable arms... The very text of the Second Amendment implicitly recognizes the pre-existence of the right and declares only that it 'shall not be infringed.'
> Justice Antonin Scalia (b. 1936)
> *District of Columbia v. Heller*
> June 26, 2008

"Where does that leave me? Can I sit here and say I'm going to beat the United States Supreme Court to the punch and I'm going to hold there's an incorporation here? I mean isn't that going a little beyond my pay grade?"

The prosecutor came foreword and argued his case for the State—their argument seemed to rely on the vagueness of what it means to "move."

"Mr. Aitken indicated he was moving back and forth between residences, moving in the sense of motion," I wondered if there was any other kind, "not essentially moving as opposed to moving things from one place to another. It was clear that he was living at both places, that he was visiting mom on certain occasions and he was living up in Hoboken, analogous I guess to a younger person who's living at college and also living at home. So I think that's really what the issue is here. It's a factual dispute for the jury to decide. As far as Title 18 of the USC, the federal Firearms Owners Protection Act, that only applies when someone is moving from one state to another. Clearly the evidence is here he's moving from Mount Laurel to Hoboken, both spots within the state of New Jersey, so 18 U.S.C. 926A does not apply."

In the prosecutors argument against why I shouldn't be protected by the federal statutes, he simultaneously conceded that I was moving from Mount Laurel to Hoboken—a concession that should have clearly permitted the State exemptions that read:

> NJS 2C:39-6e:
> "Nothing in subsections b., c. and d. of N.J.S.
> 2C:39-5 shall be construed to prevent a
> person... from carrying the same, in the

manner specified in subsection g. of this section, from any place of purchase to his residence or place of business, between his dwelling and his place of business, between one place of business or residence and another when moving..."

But the judge completely ignored the State's admission that I was moving from one house to another at the time I was arrested.

The motion was denied.

I had almost forgotten that Jenna was even there. She hadn't made a sound through the entire oral argument. I looked back at her. She sat there in the one conservative outfit she owned—a white silk blouse and black pencil skirt—looking confused; like she didn't know if she should be disappointed or hopeful, or what all of this even meant. Her curly long chestnut hair framed her lightly freckled skin and hazel gold-flecked eyes—she belonged on the beaches of Point Reyes or in the wild of Yellowstone where the air smells of untamed saltwater and damp Douglas-fir. Her free spirit belonged almost anywhere but there—surrounded by oppressive wood-paneled walls and malicious self-serving intent. Jenna flashed me an optimistic smile and I turned around as I heard the judge's voice from behind me.

"In fairness to the defendant I do think he should be given an opportunity to reconsider his rejection of the plea offer. I will give the defendant two weeks from today to inform the

Court and Mr. Brennan whether he wishes to take advantage of that offer."

With my trial date set and all attempts of having the case thrown out exhausted, the judge pushed for me to reconsider taking a plea deal.

I'd never heard of a judge extending a plea offer before—that's one of the things prosecutors do; not judges. I was under the impression that judges didn't get involved in negotiating plea deals at all. I thought they were supposed to remain neutral and not attempt to influence a trial, but Judge Morley seemed to really want me to take the deal.

The offer was the same as always: accept a five-year sentence with a one-year mandatory period of incarceration before becoming eligible for parole. I had already turned this same offer down almost a half-dozen times. But this time they wanted me to sign a piece of paper acknowledging that this was the last plea-deal I was ever going to be offered.

"You don't have to sign it now, they're giving you two weeks to think it over." Richard said, showing me the plea cutoff form.

"I'm not taking a deal, Richard. I've told you before: No deals."

He looked me in the eyes and, unlike the judge, didn't seem disappointed in me.

"I know, Brian."

"Well, let's sign it now and get it over with." I said, borrowing a pen from Richard.

Richard handed the judge the signed cutoff form and told him I had no intention of confessing to a crime I did not commit. Morley looked down at me, seemingly pissed that I kept refusing to accept a plea deal and appearing even angrier that I had been on Freedomwatch to talk about my case.

"This trial, Mr. Aitken, is not going to be a referendum on the Second Amendment."

Judge Morley chided me about how FOX News was just using me as a pawn in their news cycle and that he was trying to help me—to save me from myself and from the media.

Coming from the guy who told me it was "no big deal" for me to do a year in prison, I had a hard time believing him.

CHAPTER SIX

To say May 27, 2010 started off like any other day would be a lie.

I managed to get a full night's sleep the night before, but it wasn't peaceful. It was more like the sleep a soldier forces himself to get in the middle of combat, knowing an attack from the enemy could come at any moment. I thought of my high-school friends deployed overseas in places they weren't allowed to talk about and was glad my personal battles were in a stuffy courtroom instead of the hills of Afghanistan.

I'd spent months preparing for this day and had assured myself that I would be fine regardless of the outcome, so I remained confident when I walked into the Burlington County Courthouse for my long-awaited trial that first morning. After already experiencing what Judge Morley considered "justice," I wasn't exactly optimistic. I wasn't as nervous as my family, or Jenna, but I'd be lying if I didn't admit there was a knot twisting in my stomach.

Faced with the prospect of spending at least three years in one of New Jersey's prisons I found myself wondering what would happen if I just walked away. It couldn't be that difficult to flee the country and create a new life somewhere else, maybe Switzerland or New Zealand, a place with lots of mountains and a little more respect for freedom. Frank Abagnale made it look easy until he got caught by the Feds. But, I hadn't counterfeited millions of dollars worth of bad checks and I doubted anyone would even bother to come looking for me. My name would probably just be added to a long list of fugitives on the run. I can't imagine I'm the only person facing real time to think, briefly, about making a run for it. Anyone who's been there and tells you otherwise is lying.

I gambled my future on Richard's ability to get the facts—and the exemptions—in front of the jury, and in their ability to see the truth. By the time trial came around, I had all but given up on any expectation of a fair trial. This was a gun-grabbing show of power with a directive that came straight from the attorney general. I just hoped the jury would see the lengths the police, prosecutor, and judge went to in order to guarantee a conviction.

The only real strategy we had, if you can even call it that, was to get as much of the truth on the record as possible. I was pretty confident that I'd be acquitted of all of the charges after the jury heard about the moving exemptions and all of my efforts to comply with State and Federal gun laws—not the least of which included my phone call to the State Police, just days before my arrest, where I was told by a Trooper how to transport my firearms. Even still, as I walked into the courthouse, placing my fate in the hands of twelve strangers, I wondered what was riskier: staying and fighting an enemy I knew was more interested in getting a conviction than the truth, or taking my chances on the lam.

The courtroom was filled with my family and friends. This was the closest we'd come to a family reunion in years.

The judge ordered the jury to come in.

"Folks, will you remain standing when you get to your places, please? There's going to be an empty chair and I'll explain that to you in a minute. Each of you raise your right hand, please," Judge Morley said before swearing them in as jurors.

"Thank you, folks," Morley continued, peering down the nose of his glasses at the twelve strangers before him, "please have a seat. Juror Number Four had a problem develop in connection with his employment. So, he was excused. We're going to go with the alternate, Juror 13."

We were off to a bad start.

Richard and I both thought Juror Number Four might be sympathetic towards what happened to me and, in a courtroom, every compassionate juror counts. It turned out he worked the nightshift and didn't get to bed before 3 or 4 o'clock in the morning—something he didn't think to bring up during jury selection. Had he mentioned it, he would have been excused and my lawyer could have tried his best to get a sympathetic replacement.

Selecting the jury had been a long, drawn out, pain in the ass. Potential jurors were asked a series of various questions to find out if they leaned liberal or conservative. My lawyer tried to weed out the Democrats, while the State politely discarded anyone remotely resembling a Republican. A favorite question—since the lawyers weren't allowed to directly ask what their political beliefs were—was to ask, "what kind of bumper stickers do you have on your car?"

Anyone who answered "Bush for President," "Obama 2008," "NRA," or "The Sierra Club" were pretty much outright disqualified by one lawyer or the other. In a criminal trial, all twelve jurors must unanimously agree to the verdict. Losing Juror Number Four could be devastating if the jury wound up needing a swing vote to turn the tide in my favor.

The judge sealed the swearing in of the jury with a final statement that would come back to haunt us all.

"With the taking of the oath, ladies and gentlemen, you are now the jury in this case. As you know, this is a criminal case... You are the sole judges of the facts. Your determination of the facts is to be based solely upon the evidence submitted during the course of the trial. You should not conclude that because I rule one way or another that I have any feelings about the outcome of the case. I do not. But, even if I did, you would have to disregard them since you will be the sole judges of the facts."

The seriousness of the situation set in all at once as the judge read the charges against me. All eyes were on me. I could hear the whispers that would decide my fate over the deafening tick of the clock.

"Brian Aitken stands before you charged with the crimes of unlawful possession of weapons and possession of prohibited weapons or devices," Morley read calmly—*almost* disinterested, "The indictment is not evidence of the defendant's guilt of the charges. The defendant has pleaded not guilty to the charges and is presumed to be innocent and unless each and every essential element of an offense charged is proved beyond a reasonable doubt, the defendant must be found not guilty of that charge."

From his bench he explained that the prosecution had to prove its case by more than a mere preponderance of the evidence but not necessarily to a degree of absolute certainty. The State had to prove I was guilty "beyond a reasonable doubt"—if the jury held any doubt in their mind that I could be innocent, they must find me not guilty. I thought the fact that I had complied with the State and Federal exemptions was more than enough to create a reasonable doubt in the jurors' eyes. I was confident that, given the chance to weigh the evidence and consider the exemptions, I would be acquitted. Two motions rooted in common sense had already been quashed by this judge and I couldn't help but feel like the trial was rigged.

"In this world," Morley continued, "we know very few things with absolute certainty. In criminal cases, the law does not require proof that overcomes every possible doubt. If, based on your consideration of the evidence, you are firmly convinced that the defendant is guilty of the crime charged, you must find him guilty. If on the other hand, you are not firmly convinced of his guilt, you must give him the benefit of the doubt and find him not guilty." The judge handed the stage to the prosecutor for his opening argument.

"Thank you, Judge Morley. Good morning everybody. I know you're anxious to find out what the case is about, so I'll spare you the pleasantries and we'll get right to work." Brennan said, his balding frame drowning in a suit two sizes too big.

"Let me start with the obvious. Handguns are a serious matter. They're deadly weapons. They can kill people," Brennan went for the heartstrings right off the bat, "The State of New Jersey has stated that, by Legislation requiring anyone carrying a handgun, and that's the keyword 'Carrying a handgun in the State of New Jersey,' needs to get a permit to do so.

And by carrying, they mean carrying it around on your person or driving with it in your car about the roads and highways of the State. You do not need a permit to have a gun in your home or on your property.

This case is about Mr. Aitken carrying a handgun. And every person who carries a handgun in New Jersey, with some very strict and narrow exceptions that we'll talk about in a minute, needs to get a permit."

And then Brennan said something unexpected. He started weaving his fan-fiction into the facts, hoping it would make his fantasy believable.

"He was driving from his apartment in Northern New Jersey to his mother's home in Mount Laurel. Now, the evidence will show that the reason for him traveling there was that an Ocean County Court had granted Mr. Aitken visitation of his son in Toms River."

Just a few months earlier during his argument against my Motion to Dismiss, he passionately contended that I was "clearly moving between Mount Laurel and Hoboken"— now his story was that I was coming down to Mount Laurel, 90 miles south of Hoboken, to see my son two days later and 45 miles in the other direction.

It didn't make any sense.

Brennan clearly didn't bother to look at a map of New Jersey when he chose that argument—and he must have been hoping the jury had poor geography skills. Toms River was located halfway between Hoboken and Mount Laurel and, not once, had I ever gone to pick up my mother. Every single time we met in Toms River, each driving our own cars and meeting in the parking lot of the library. But, as the judge mentioned in his opening statement to the jury, the prosecutor isn't necessarily telling the truth—or submitting evidence—during his opening statement. He's just spinning the story he wants the jury to believe. He's supposed to present evidence to support this version of the facts but, in this case, he never did. That didn't stop him from trying, though.

"Now, I briefly mentioned exemptions to the rule. These exemptions are narrow and carved out of the statute for particular reasons. For instance, law enforcement officers don't need a permit to carry a handgun. You don't need a permit to carry a handgun from the gun store to your home. You don't need a permit to drive the gun to the shooting range, as long as it's being carried properly. So, there are exemptions to the rule.

And, one of the exemptions that they're going to latch onto is to suggest that Mr. Aitken was justified in this particular situation because he was moving. Now, in the law in New

Jersey, there is an exception to the rule for a permit saying that if you're moving from one place to another, obviously, you have to get the gun there somehow, correct? It makes sense.

This isn't about registering a gun. You don't need to register a gun in the State of New Jersey. So, don't be confused about that. You don't need to register it. But, if you're going to carry it, you need a permit.

So, Mr. Aitken was not moving. I mean, it's all going to come down to what you consider to be 'moving'."

Truer words were never spoken. And here I was, thinking Newton had already taken care of that for all of us.

"It's simply an attempt to get a square peg into a round hole. All Mr. Aitken was doing on the date and time in question was trying to circumvent the permit rules of the State of New Jersey. If he's guilty of the offenses, we ask you hold him accountable. Thank you."

For the first time, Brennan had laid his game plan in front of us and I felt like I had before—when I was in family court—trying to disprove a story that had no facts to support it in the first place. I remember that moment like it was yesterday. That was the moment I stopped believing in the system.

In Richard's opening remarks he argued that the prosecutor couldn't avoid acknowledging that the laws in New Jersey provide exemptions for law-abiding citizens to get their firearms from Point A to Point B.

"Now, let's talk about the charges a little bit," Richard started, wearing his ridiculously loud chili-pepper tie, "Mr. Aitken is accused of possessing his own property. He's not accused of misusing it in any way. He is not accused of possessing it on his person where it's immediately accessible. He is not accused of threatening anyone with it, harming anyone with it, or doing anything nefarious with it. This is property that he lawfully purchased—and the State will acknowledge this as the trial goes on.

Mr. Aitken did everything correct when he bought his handguns in Colorado. He bought them from licensed dealers. One of them was Bass Pro Shops, you might have heard of them. He voluntarily underwent a Federal background check and a State background check and he bought them from licensed dealers. He didn't buy them from a friend or a friend of a friend or some guy off the street."

I thought Gilbert masterfully explained to the jury that at the time I was arrested I had three residences: a home in Colorado, a room at my parents' house, and a recently reacquired apartment in Hoboken.

"The State has been relentless in its prosecution of Mr. Aitken and I can't tell you why. I don't know. But, I can tell you this: They cannot prove that he violated New Jersey State law, because he complied with it every step of the way.

Thank you."

Naturally, Brennan objected to my lawyers opening statement but he seemed mostly unfazed when he called his first witness: Mount Laurel Patrolman Michael Joy.

Brennan's line of questioning was straightforward. He intended to show that my guns were dangerous and deadly, in an attempt to make the jurors believe that I too, was dangerous and deadly.

"What's the difference between hollow-point ammunition and full metal jacket ammunition?" Brennan asked Officer Joy.

"Full metal jacket just means that the projectile itself is encased in copper and hollow-point bullets have a hole in the top of the bullet, so whenever it hits anything, the bullet expands and creates more damage than a full metal jacket bullet."

"And is hollow-point ammunition legal?"

"Not in New Jersey."

"Why is that?"

"It's against the law."

Richard objected.

"Objection, again, Judge. Now he's making a legal

conclusion, and an incorrect one, I might add."

The judge ordered the jury out of the courtroom.

"It's a fact that hollow-point ammunition is illegal in New Jersey," the prosecutor argued—ignoring the fact that anyone with a valid permit to purchase in New Jersey could buy hollow-point ammunition at their local Dick's Sporting Goods. Or, like me, they could move it legally into the state without any permit—so long as they weren't prohibited from owning firearms.

"Well," the judge asked, "the objection came at the point where the witness testified that the purpose of hollow-point ammunition is to do more damage at the point of contact. I mean, is that appropriate testimony from this witness and, secondly, is it relevant?"

"Well," Brennan responded, "I think it's relevant to distinguish it from ball ammunition and to say why it's illegal."

The judge ordered the jury back into the courtroom and told them to disregard any reason why the ammunition might be illegal—all they needed to know was that the ammunition *was* illegal and that if they determined I possessed it, I must be found guilty.

Conveniently, the fact that hollow-point ammunition wasn't illegal was left out, again.

Brennan then admitted each handgun as evidence, taking his time while questioning Officer Joy about the guns and how semi-automatic handguns work. He did the same with the ammunition, lingering on adjectives like "deadly" and "dangerous".

Every kind of ammunition retrieved from my locked trunk was broken down into little plastic bags and admitted separately, giving the appearance that I had been traveling with enough ammo to storm the beaches at Normandy. It was a cheap parlor trick—but an effective one.

The prosecutor then had Officer Joy take one of the magazines from my car and load it on the stand, counting each bullet as he snapped them into place. Then, each kind of ammunition was passed out to the jury so they could see these deadly instruments of war with their own eyes.

This wasn't a trial. It was theater.

Throughout the rest of the trial Judge Morley would allow every piece of physical evidence the prosecution submitted —but refused to admit even a single piece of physical evidence that supported my innocence.

"As I told Mr. Aitken long before you were in the case," Morley said, "this is not going to be a referendum on New Jersey law and whether New Jersey laws are a good or bad idea."

In one of the scariest decisions Judge Morley made, he chose to interpret the Federal Exemption—the one that allows law-abiding gun owners to travel safely from one state to another with their guns—as not applying to ammunition or magazines. He decided that only firearms without their magazines are protected by that law.

It's terrifying to think how many innocent people could be made felons overnight for interpreting a law differently than a judge might. Every single gun owner I have ever asked has told me they believe that the law allows them to transport their magazines with their firearms. If they came across the wrong police officer and the wrong judge in the wrong state, they'd suddenly find themselves on the wrong side of the "ignorance of the law is no excuse" argument.

And that's a bad place to be.

My lawyer spoke up while the jury was sequestered, again. "Your Honor you've indicated at various points that hollow-points here are illegal. Well, under the statute, there are exemptions for that, too. And they're not illegal under every circumstance. I would just ask Your Honor to be careful as to how you phrase that because I don't want the jury picking up on your words that automatically classify them as illegal when they're not."

"I'll tell them that as well."

"Thank you, Judge."

The jury was brought back in.

"Ladies and gentlemen, two things. Number one, earlier I believe I made a statement about hollow-point bullets being illegal in New Jersey. There are exceptions to the prohibition on possessing hollow-point bullets. There are exceptions. If, based on the evidence as it's presented, the defendant is entitled to argue that he was covered by one of the exceptions, I will let you know. Okay? If I left you with the impression that hollow-point ammunition is in all instances illegal in New Jersey, that's incorrect.

Second thing I need to tell you is that the State and the defendant agree that Mr. Aitken lawfully acquired and possessed the three handguns in the State of Colorado. Okay? Thank you, folks. Can we continue?"

Officer Joy went on to testify that my car was packed full of duffel bags, boxes, and backpacks and that I had just moved back from Colorado a week before he arrested me. And that neither he, nor anyone else, ever believed I had been living permanently in New Jersey for the past six months. He also testified that he listed the length of my residence in the community as only being six days when submitting a special form to a judge to determine my suitability for bail. Joy had implied that I should not be provided bail because I hadn't lived in New Jersey long enough, and could be a flight risk.

This, of course, contradicted the State's very argument that I had completed my move from Colorado half a year earlier.

"Officer Joy," Richard asked on his cross-examination, "when you went to the family home, you were told that there had been an argument, correct?"

"Yes."

"And you were told that the argument was verbal only and that no one had been hurt, correct?"

"Correct."

"And, in fact, the caller hung up the phone before anyone at dispatch answered, is that right?"

"Yes."

"Now, you indicated earlier that Mr. Aitken had told you he had just moved back from Colorado, right?"

"Yes."

"And, also, his mother indicated to you that he had just moved back from Colorado, correct?"

"Yes."

"And after speaking with his Mom, you were aware that he was living between his parents' house there in Mount Laurel, as well as his apartment in Hoboken, correct?"

"Well, his main residence was up in Hoboken, as far as I knew."

"And you called him on the phone and asked him to come back?"

"Yes."

"Okay. And he denied to you that he was suicidal in any way, right?"

"Yes."

"Okay. And at first, he didn't want to come back did he?"

"Not really."

"And, so, you told him that if he didn't come back, you would put out a statewide alert for him, correct?"

"We already put out the state wide alert for him."

"And based on his second conversation with you, he decided to turn around and come back, correct?"

"Yes."

It was too late for Fourth Amendment arguments. The time to suppress the evidence because I was threatened and intimidated with incarceration, even though they had no probable cause to suspect me of a crime, had come and gone. Still, Richard was trying to get as much on the record as possible, preserving the truth just in case we needed to appeal.

"And after Brian returned and you patted him down you spoke with him for a while, correct?"

"Yes."

"And that conversation actually lasted over an hour, didn't it?"

"Approximately, I guess."

"And during that time, Brian was not free to leave, was he?"

"Not until the investigation was through."

As both Josselson and Gilbert had explained to me before, this was one of the major things that was horribly wrong with how the police treated me. It is illegal to hold someone against their will if there is no belief that person has committed, or is on their way to commit, a crime.

"Now let me just change subjects for a moment. And I just want to be certain that I understand correctly here. Regarding the firearms, sitting here today, you indicated that you did not do any tests on the firearms, right?"

"No, I didn't."

"So, you do not know if those firearms work, do you?"

"No."

"And you also indicated that you did no tests on the

ammunition or magazines, correct?"

"Correct."

"And, so, you cannot sit here and tell us that any of those magazines will continuously and directly feed more than 15 rounds into a semiautomatic firearm, can you?'

"No."

"All right. So, just a recap, you responded to the house for the 9-1-1 call, right?"

"Yes."

"You were told that Mr. Aitken might be suicidal?"

"Yes."

"And you were concerned for him?"

"Yes."

"So you called him back to the house?"

"Yes."

"And, then you took him to the hospital?"

"No."

"And, in fact, you never took Mr. Aitken to the hospital, did you?"

"No."

"Instead, you searched his trunk and arrested him, right?"

Joy fidgeted in his chair and tried to find the words around the truth: he didn't give a damn about me; he was told I owned guns and he wanted the glory of taking me down for it.

"There were other officers there with you at the scene, right?"

"Yes."

"Do you recall one of the other officers handing Mr. Aitken's firearms back to his parents?"

"I don't remember. That wasn't me, though."

Joy was excused and a recess was called while the prosecution called their next witness: my mother.

"The State calls Susan Aitken," Prosecutor John Brennan called to the court.

Watching my mother being sworn in was horrifying. No boy grows up hoping that one day, they'll watch their mother take the stand as a witness against him in a felony trial. My mother was the most caring person I'd ever met and she didn't love anyone or anything as much as she loved my brother, sister, and me. This was my lowest point as a son, and she just didn't deserve the attack she was about to receive from the prosecutor.

"Did you think Brian was going to harm himself?" Brennan started, softly, trying to build camaraderie with my mother over his fictional concern for my well being.

"I was concerned about that. That's why I called 9-1-1."

"And how did you think he was going to harm himself?"

"Maybe a knife, I don't know, pills. I don't know."

"But, you never told the police anything about guns?"

"I'm not sure if I did. I mean, I may have. I'm not positive." My mom wasn't trying to dodge the question. She gets overwhelmed in moments of stress and anxiety and it's very difficult for her to remember things. I knew this about her, and so did the rest of my family, but the jury didn't.

"Now, when this happened, was your son living in Hoboken?"

"I think he was living in Hoboken. He stayed with us. Well, he was back and forth. I'm not sure exactly where he was *living* living."

"Somewhere in North Jersey?"

"Yes, I think he was still moving."

"And he had been living there for some months, correct?" Brennan asked, ignoring that my mom had just said I was moving in an effort to get her to confirm a statement she didn't make.

"I'm not sure how many months. He came back quite a few times from Colorado and was staying with us for part of the time and was staying with a friend for part of the time and going back to Colorado, back and forth."

My mom's phone vibrated and the judge ripped into her for not shutting off her phone in his courtroom.

"But, the sign said to put it on vibrate," she said meekly, fumbling through her purse to turn off the phone.

She was a mess.

"Okay," Brennan said, getting back on track. "Was he coming to your house on this occasion to take you to Toms River for visitation with his son, Logan?"

"He was coming, moving some things back to the house and we were going to visitation."

I don't think my mom realized the prosecutor was asking why I was coming down on that particular day and not what our plans were for the weekend.

Brennan moved to enter my Parenting Time Order into evidence. He had been trying all day to establish my residency as being exclusively in New Jersey and not also in Colorado because I had a Court Ordered visitation schedule to see my son once a week. But without that schedule I wouldn't have any established right to see my son. Living in another state wouldn't nullify the visitation agreement. I would still have the right to see my son in New Jersey even if I lived in a different state—or even a different country. But the prosecution wanted to admit the visitation order as proof that I was a legal resident of New Jersey as of November 14 —and not late December, a few days before I was arrested, as Officer Joy had already testified.

The judge allowed the family court order—a piece of paper my mother had never seen before that morning when the prosecutor showed it to her—to be entered into evidence through my mother's testimony.

I didn't even see what the big deal was. It hardly seemed like a damning piece of evidence that I had a visitation agreement to see my son. In no way did I think the Order proved I lived in New Jersey, like the prosecutor said it did. My son lived in New Jersey, that was all.

The judge had the parenting-time order marked into evidence and Brennan continued his direct examination of my mother, "Prior to the Court getting involved, was Brian having visitation with Logan?"

"I think he saw him a few times when she would allow and when he was available."

"And was he living in North Jersey at the time?"

"At what time?"

I had been moving around so much my mom couldn't even keep track. After answering too generally earlier, and having Brennan contort her words, she wanted to be as specific as possible.

"The time prior to November, when you said there was prior visitation, where were the respective parties living at that time?"

"Lea lived with us for a while. Then, she moved back to her home in Toms River. Brian went back to Colorado and was there for the majority of the time, came back to Mount Laurel, back and forth."

"Was Brian flying from Colorado every weekend from mid-November until January of 2009?"

"Not every weekend."

"How many weekends would he fly in?"

"Twice, and he drove."

"Now you testified earlier that you didn't see guns on this date, correct?"

"On January 2nd?"

"Yes."

"No, actually, I did see guns."

"Okay. Where did you see guns?"

"When the police officers brought them to my house to give them back to me."

"Now, you didn't recall that this morning," Brennan said, trying to discredit my mom, as if she was making it up.

"Oh, no, I did not, because you were talking about my son. I never saw my son in possession of guns ever."

Brennan told the jury that I must have been driving around with guns in my car for weeks on end because my mother never saw me take them out of her house and put them in my car. I've never met a single person who made a public show of moving their firearms around. Every responsible gun owner I knew moved his or her firearms as discretely as possible.

But Brennan's only job was to convict me, no matter how ridiculous the story he had to weave.

Watching my mother being questioned on the stand was one of the most difficult things I've ever witnessed. She told the truth and did a good job avoiding the many traps Brennan placed for her, but still, my heart broke watching her on the stand. Witnessing my own lawyer cross-examine her wasn't much easier.

"Between June and December of 2008, how many more times did Brian come back to visit you?" my lawyer asked.

"From Colorado?"

"Yes, let's start with that."

"Probably three times," my mother answered.

"And at some point during this period Brian also got an apartment in Hoboken and started hunting for a job in New York City, correct?"

"Yes."

"So, during this period, Brian was in the process of moving back and forth between Colorado, Mount Laurel, and Hoboken?"

"Yes."

My mom testified that I had personal possessions in all three residences and, on the day of my arrest, many of those possessions were in my car. Including towels, sheets, and kitchen plates. Richard was laying the groundwork for both the Federal and State exemptions and the testimony couldn't be clearer: I was moving. It was messy, there was a divorce— I lived in different places alternating at different times, trying to save my job and my relationship with my son thousands of miles away.

"And after the police discussed the issue with Brian and removed the firearms from his trunk, did you observe what they did with those firearms?"

"Yes."

"What did they do?"

"They brought them to my front door and knocked on the door and asked if I had somewhere to keep them."

"And, at that time, did they indicate that they were going to arrest Brian?"

"No."

Richard then produced the closing documents from the sale of my house to have them marked into evidence. I had sold my house in Colorado on January 13, 2009—eleven days after I was arrested. I thought this was more convincing of my dual-state residency than my visitation order, but the judge didn't see it that way. Even though my mother identified my signature, just as she had done to verify the authenticity of the prosecutor's evidence, the judge wouldn't allow it to be entered as evidence.

The court wasn't going to allow anything that favored my defense.

And with that, the prosecution rested their case.

CHAPTER SEVEN

I could hardly believe that the State had argued and rested its case before we even broke for lunch. How could they be that confident?

Brennan and my lawyer approached the judge after the jury left for recess. Gilbert spoke first, "I'm aware that Your Honor has determined that my client's house closing documents may not get in, but..."

"I haven't ruled that," the judge interrupted, "my ruling was that you can't get something in evidence simply by having somebody who has never seen something read what that document is and then get it in. Why are you pointing in Mr. Brennan's direction?"

"Isn't that what just occurred with the Civil Action Order

regarding Mr. Aitken's parenting time?"

"Actually, no," Morley shot back, "what else did you have?"

"Okay," Richard calmly replied, "at this time, the defense would make a motion to dismiss the State's case."

"All right, go for it."

"Well, first off, as to count one and all of the counts, unless I missed it, I don't recall Officer Joy identifying Mr. Aitken on the record. I do not recall him identifying that it was Mr. Aitken that he took the firearms from. I do not remember him making a visual identification of Mr. Aitken at all."

It was a shot in the dark—no pun intended—and, not surprisingly, the judge denied it. With that out of the way Richard made his real argument: the State hadn't met their burden of proof.

"With count two, regarding the large capacity magazines, I believe the State has clearly failed to meet the elements of the offense."

"Which elements?" the judge questioned.

"Well, 2C:39-1(y) defines a large capacity ammunition magazine to mean a box, drum, tube, or other container which is capable of holding more than 15 rounds of ammunition to be fed continuously and directly therefrom into a semiautomatic firearm. Now, Officer Joy performed absolutely no tests on the magazine. He did not indicate that it continuously fed any ammunition into any kind of firearm. The State has to prove this beyond a reasonable doubt and the State simply has not done any tests to show that the magazine fits, (a) into a semiautomatic firearm or (b) actually feeds continuously and directly therefrom into the semiautomatic firearm.

Without any kind of tests, the State has failed to meet the elements of the offense. It's important that we meet the elements of the statute because only certain magazines are banned under New Jersey law. A magazine that holds 100 rounds and feeds into a fully automatic firearm is legal under New Jersey law. It is not banned."

"What's your authority for that?"

"Well, the statute itself, because it has to feed continuously and directly therefrom into a semiautomatic firearm. Semiautomatic. That's different from automatic. It's different from lever action. It's different from bolt action."

"Well, that's interesting but I don't know that I need to know all of that."

"And the State hasn't proved that the magazines work. They must work or else they are not illegal."

"Judge," the prosecutor interrupted, "the State doesn't have to prove that it works. The State is entitled to all reasonable inferences. You prove that by looking at it with your eyeballs, and that's all we have to prove."

"You don't have to prove that it was operable? That the magazine would function?" Morley asked the prosecutor.

"No, Judge. There's no authority that we have to have testing done on the high capacity ammunition magazine."

Judge Morley eyed my lawyer, "Did you have authority for that proposition, Mr. Gilbert?"

"Respectfully, Judge, I do. The black and white letter of the statute that says, 'Any other container which is capable of holding more than 15 rounds to be fed continuously and directly therefrom into a semiautomatic firearm.'

That means it has to be capable of firing it. Let me give the Court another example. The Tommy gun that we all know from war movies comes in two versions. There's a fully automatic version and there's a semiautomatic version. The magazines look like they interchange, but they don't. The catches at the back of the magazine are different shapes. And a magazine for a fully automatic Thompson will not fit and function in a semiautomatic Thompson. Why is this important?

It's important because not every magazine may work in every gun and the magazine has to work in a semiautomatic firearm and the State has not met that element."

It seemed like we were arguing a technicality... but the technicality favored my innocence, at least for the charge of illegal possession of high-capacity magazines. I looked back at Jenna and my parents. They seemed tired and out of place. I was glad they were there and wished they weren't, that they didn't *have* to be, all at the same time.

We were witnessing a Kafkaesque waste of time and money. I hadn't hurt anyone and the younger, naïve, me couldn't understand what anyone could possibly have to gain by throwing me in prison.

Morley denied the motion to dismiss the high-capacity magazine charge. But our resistance made it onto the record.

Gilbert went on to try and have the last charge, Illegal Possession of Hollow Point Ammunition, dismissed because the State—in thousands of pages of legislation—never actually defined what hollow-points are.

"I don't even think we have a clear definition in the statute of what a 'hollow nose or dum dum bullet' is. I mean, historically speaking, I know a dum dum bullet comes from the Ishapore Armory in India," my lawyer argued.

"I saw that on Wikipedia this morning," Judge Morley replied.

Great.

Denied.

Denied. Denied. Denied.

Judge Morley wasn't allowing a single piece of evidence in to support my innocence and he didn't seem to care if the State met its burden in meeting the elements of the charges they levied against me. You would think that when a man is facing up to ten years in prison for a non-violent and victimless crime, the legislators would want as many safeguards in place as possible to protect that person from wrongful incarceration. But, in the courtroom, there is no higher authority than the judge. And he wasn't allowing anything that might get me off the hook.

Richard called the third and final witness of the day: my best friend Michael Torrice.

Mike is the kind of guy who will do just about anything to help out a friend, so long as it didn't compromise his morals. He inherited his mother's good Christian nature, and wouldn't lie for anyone. He made that clear to me when I asked him to testify—and I told him to "just tell the truth."

Mike answered the prosecutor's questions one by one. He knew that I had personal possessions in our shared apartment in Hoboken as well as in Colorado and Mount Laurel—where my parents lived—and I was living back and forth between all three residences. I remember those months very vividly. I was trying to figure out my entire life and I had no idea where I might wind up permanently, I just knew I wanted to be there for my son and that I had bills to pay.

"Before Brian moved back from Colorado to New Jersey, did you observe him do any research on New Jersey firearm laws?" my lawyer, Richard, asked Mike, dressed like the student-lawyer he was.

"Yeah, there was a point when we were in the car and he had called the New Jersey State Police and he had a conversation with an Officer."

"Judge, I'm going to object to that." Brennan spoke up.

"Well, he was in a car and he called the New Jersey State Police. You're objecting to that?" the judge asked.

"Yes."

"Well, what's your objection, that he made a phone call?"

"I mean, it's hearsay. It's a self-serving statement."

"Well, he can testify to what he heard. He heard Mr. Aitken make a phone call. I'm not sure that he can testify as to whom the phone call was made, unless he heard something from Mr. Aitken."

"Well, I'm objecting to anything that Mr. Aitken said, because it's offered by the defense as a self-serving statement, which is not allowed."

I had called the State Police just days before moving while sitting in the passenger seat of Mike's Jeep and asked them what I had to do in order to move my firearms legally. Mike watched me make the phone call and heard every word. Richard wanted to show I made every good-faith effort to comply with the State law as possible but, again, the judge would not admit any evidence that might prove my innocence.

The judge addressed the jury.

"Ok. Ladies and gentlemen, to the extent that this witness has testified to whom Mr. Aitken was making the telephone call, you must disregard that. That's hearsay. The witness is not entitled to testify to what somebody else told him, if it's being offered to prove that fact."

"So, Your Honor," my lawyer began, "if I understand your ruling correctly, then, if he visually observed something, that may be different. That may be something that you would permit?"

"If he saw him dial a particular number, he can tell the Jury what number was being dialed. If he saw something on a readout, perhaps, depending on what it is that he saw on the readout. Go ahead."

Richard looked at me and then turned his attention back to Mike.

"At any point, Mr. Torrice, did you observe any New Jersey statutes in Brian Aitken's hand?"

"Yes, on the computer and also printed out."

"And did you happen to notice what those statutes were about?"

"Yeah, they were about New Jersey Gun Laws and, basically, how to transport firearms."

Finally.

I felt like if the judge hadn't just explicitly said he would allow something Mike saw than he would never allow any evidence that showed I'd researched the transportation laws in New Jersey. Immediately after my phone call with the Detective from the Belmar State Police barracks, I went on to the website the Trooper told me to go to and printed out the detailed laws explaining how to transport everything.

I made sure I followed the law to the letter.

From my arrest through the grand jury proceedings and into the trial, the prosecution had tried to show that I was transporting firearms without a concealed-carry permit. But this wholly ignored the exemptions to the law that allow a person to transport their legally owned firearms between one house and another without a permit. I was moving my guns from Mount Laurel to Hoboken and everyone had testified to that—even Officer Joy. Thankfully, no special permit was required because concealed carry permits (CCP) are notoriously difficult for law-abiding citizens to get in New

Jersey.

The State of New Jersey requires citizens to prove they have a "justifiable need" to get a carry permit. In America, most states are "shall issue" states, which means if you're a law-abiding citizen and request a CCP the State *shall* issue it. New Jersey is different. New Jersey and a handful of other states are *may* issue States—which means they might give you one if they feel like it. And, unless you're part of an 'elite few', they don't.

New Jersey's restrictive scheme to keep people from legally carrying firearms concealed has been questioned by nineteen other states because it is nearly impossible to prove the subjective "justifiable need" standard. In one instance, a New Jersey shop owner who had been kidnapped, beaten, and robbed was denied a concealed carry permit. He was scared for his life but, in New Jersey, that's still not enough to prove you need to carry a firearm for self-defense outside of your home. New Jersey's system is so ridiculous that even retired law-enforcement officers can't get a permit to carry. Most permits go to politicians and the well-connected.

The prosecutor's cross-examination of Mike was relentless. At times, Brennan was practically yelling at Mike for not giving him the answer he wanted, or for asking the prosecutor to clarify a question.

"Now, you seem to be suggesting that Brian's in this constant state of moving, right? Now, where was he moving to? Was he just moving back and forth or was he going somewhere?"

"Well, yeah," Mike answered respectfully, "it was different places at different times."

"But where was his ultimate destination?"

"At which time?"

"Well, the time you just testified to. Where was he going? What was he doing?"

"At what point in time?"

"Well, you're using the word "moving" repeatedly."

"Uh-huh."

"Right? Where is he moving to?"

"Well, he moved from Colorado to Mount Laurel, from Mount Laurel to Hoboken. From Hoboken back to Mount Laurel. I mean, these were all separate moves."

"Well, what, did he like take a sock each trip or something? How much stuff would he take?"

"A carload, as much as he could."

"Just back and forth?"

"When he moved from one place to another, yes."

"So, he wasn't actually moving in a sense of moving residences. He's moving between them?"

"Each time, he was changing where he was residing."

Brennan was growing livid.

"Well, what does moving out mean to you?" he antagonized.

"Well, I mean, it's a process. I've moved several times when I was in college. Until I had all of my possessions from one place to another, I wouldn't have considered it to be done."

"So, you're telling us that he was in a constant state of moving from September of 2008, right?"

"Yes."

"It's your testimony that from the time he got there in September, he was in a constant state of moving to where?"

"In September he was moving to Hoboken. Once he moved in, and that whole time, he still had possessions in Colorado. Then he was moving back to Mount Laurel from Hoboken and then..."

Brennan cut him off again, "to do what?!?"

"I... I don't know."

"He wasn't physically moving out of Hoboken, was he?"

"Yes, he was!"

Mike's a pretty patient guy but Brennan was asking him the same question a thousand different ways trying to trip him up. He couldn't possibly have been any clearer.

"And the reason he was living in Hoboken was because he was working in New York?"

"And the reason he was moving out was because he no longer worked there," Mike replied, growing tired of Brennan's antics.

"But, he had established himself in New York?"

"And he was working there, yes. He established himself in my apartment in Hoboken and then he was leaving."

Mike was excused and court was adjourned for the day.

I was exhausted, physically and emotionally, but it wasn't over. Not yet. We still had one more witness to call: my father.

CHAPTER EIGHT

My dad grew up in a rough neighborhood in Germantown —the West side of Philadelphia—in the sixties. He was the youngest of eight, raised by a strong-willed Irish-catholic mother and a hardworking father who put himself through college while laboring full-time as a chemist for the city of Philadelphia and supporting a family of ten. My grandfather studied on the bus ride to and from work, and eventually taught at Temple University.

I think that's where my father and I get our work ethic from.

When I was sixteen, my dad took me to my first concert. Aerosmith had come to town, riding their most recent wave of success with the release of *Armageddon*. He made me promise not to tell my mom about all the topless girls throwing their bras at the Toxic Twins. The kick of the bass drum during "Janie's Got A Gun" sent shockwaves through my body. The radio does not do that song justice.

When I was eleven, my dad used to wake up at four in the morning when the weather was absolutely horrible to help me deliver my papers. At eighteen, he bought me a Joe Perry signature Les Paul for Christmas. It had a black, flamed maple, finish and matte black hardware with Seymour Duncan Screamin' Demon humbucking pickups. I don't know if it was something he could afford. We never really worried about money, but I know he spent several months painting houses after he moved us into Mount Laurel—a family neighborhood with growing notoriety for its great school system. He had been laid off, and wasn't the type of guy to sit around and collect unemployment checks. For months he traded his suit and tie for a set of overalls, and took work wherever he could find it.

As a teenager he taught me the hard way not to curse in front of my mother. We had tickets to see Eric Clapton—my guitar idol—and, after I said a particular four-letter word in front of my mom, he took her instead. I was furious. "He's gonna die and I'm never going to see him play, dad!" I was a little dramatic...but at fifty-two years old, Clapton seemed ancient, and I wasn't sure how many years his body had left after decades of abusing hard drugs and booze.

I hated my dad for not taking me. But it was fair.

It used to scare me when people told me how alike my dad

and I are. Now, as an adult, I take it as a compliment.

+++

"This is the matter of the State of New Jersey versus Brian Aitken. Good morning to everybody. While we wait for the jury there's the issue of the defendant's father testifying in order to introduce the real estate settlement documents from Colorado."

"Yes, Judge," Richard brought the documents marked 'D6' up to the judge, who flipped through the closing documents and reviewed them from behind his bifocals.

"There's a number of documents. First page is on the letterhead of the Guardian Title Agency and is captioned Settlement Statement for a property in Broomfield, Colorado. Settlement date January 13, 2009, sellers are Brian and Lea Aitken... Now, the defendant argues that all of these documents are admissible under 8:03C-6. And the point of all of these documents is that settlement on this property in Colorado took place on January 13th, right? That's the goal here, right?"

"That's correct."

Gilbert and Morley debated whether or not my dad would be allowed to testify about the sale of my house. In the judge's eyes, anything my dad had to say about it was hearsay. He argued that only the maker of the document could introduce the document. But that's not how he felt about anything the prosecution submitted into evidence.

The double standard was alive and well.

It was my understanding that it wasn't the judge's job to argue why something can't be admitted. That's the job of the prosecution, but Judge Morley was so adamant about not admitting any evidence that might favor my innocence that he appeared to argue for the prosecution on more than one occasion. When he caught himself, he'd say "I'm not doing Mr. Brennan's work for him." Which, of course, he was.

Brennan just stood there silently while the judge did his dirty work.

"How do I know Mr. Aitken didn't just photoshop these and print them out this morning? I have no idea if this is real or who signed it," the judge said, applying infinite more scrutiny to the closing documents my dad had actually seen than the papers they had authenticated through my mother, which she had never even seen before.

Morley continued to argue that the documents weren't relevant because all they showed was that I sold my house in Colorado on January 13th and—in his opinion—that had nothing to do with the case that was being tried.

But it did.

The purpose of allowing the jury to see the closing

documents was to show them that between April of 2008 and January 13, 2009 I was involved in a complex cross-country move involving numerous people and complicated property interests. It wasn't a single and discreet move.

"Your Honor, the relevance is self-evident here. If somebody has a large house that they sell, it's incumbent upon them to remove their possessions from it, and I think it's clearly linked to the fact that Mr. Aitken was moving his possessions at the time this occurred contemporaneously with the sale of the house. The relevance is obvious, I think."

The judge refused to allow my father to testify about the settlement documents. We weren't allowed to mention them at all. However, my father was allowed to testify that he had knowledge of my intent to move from Colorado to New Jersey... but no physical evidence was allowed to support his statement. He was also specifically prohibited from talking about how he saw me moving things out of his house and into my car on January 1st and 2nd.

The jury and my father were brought in from opposite sides of the courtroom.

"At some point during the 2008 time frame what did you discuss with your son, Brian Aitken, regarding this Colorado property?" Richard asked.

"Whether to sell it or keep it."

"And when did these discussions occur?"

"Probably beginning around May, all the way through the end of the year until it eventually sold in January."

"So it eventually sold in January?"

"Yes."

"That's all I have, Your Honor."

He was only on the stand for two minutes.

I made the choice not to testify. I didn't want to give any legitimacy to this kangaroo court and felt like if I participated I was tacitly condoning the entire sham of a trial. They could force me to stand there, but they couldn't force me to dig my own grave. After watching the other witnesses, I knew the judge didn't hear what you said. He heard what the prosecutor *said* you said.

With the jury at recess, the next hour was spent debating what charges and exemptions, if any, were going to be read to the jury. The judge decided the federal Firearms Owners Protection Act wasn't going to be read—so they wouldn't even be allowed to consider it—because it didn't provide any protections that the New Jersey exemptions didn't already provide. "It's duplicative," the judge said, "do you want me to say he enjoys an exemption under New Jersey law and, by the way folks, there's the same exemption under Federal law? Exactly the same thing? Why would I do that?"

The judge decided not to tell the jury about the Federal law that protected my right to take my firearms from Colorado, just a few days earlier, to my parents house and then to Hoboken—a series of moves protected under the FOPA, which allows firearms to be transported "from any place where he may lawfully possess and carry such firearm to any other place where he may lawfully possess and carry such firearm."

The judge went on to misremember all of the testimony he witnessed that day starting with the fictitious claims that there was no evidence I had been living in Mount Laurel.

My lawyer tried to correct him, since Officer Joy, my mother —the State's own witnesses—and Mike all testified I had been living in Mount Laurel before moving back to Hoboken. But Judge Morley pretended like none of that ever happened. It seemed he had made up his mind long ago and wanted to present the jury with his version of what he thought *could* have happened, instead of what the facts showed *had* happened: that I was in a complicated move from Colorado to Mount Laurel, Mount Laurel to Hoboken, Hoboken to Mount Laurel, and Mount Laurel back to Hoboken.

The judge very matter-of-factly told my lawyer what had happened, "The evidence is that he took the guns from Hoboken and went to Mount Laurel. He added to what he had in the car. He never took the weapons out of the car and left them at Mount Laurel."

I'm not sure where he came up with that. No one said that during the trial. To the contrary, everyone testified I had gone to Mount Laurel to pack up all of my belongings. No one ever said where the guns were and no one even so much as hinted that I had them in my car before I arrived at my parents' house. I assume, because my mom didn't specifically see me walk from my old bedroom to my car with my handguns, that the judge decided they must have been in my car the entire time. But, as my mother testified, the only time she ever saw my guns were when the police officer gave them to her to bring back inside her house. Morley was jumping to conclusions and treating his own unfounded speculation as fact that wasn't supported by any evidence or testimony presented at trial.

"There's no evidence that he was residing in Mount Laurel," Morley continued. "The evidence is that he was residing in Hoboken and he was getting stuff from Mount Laurel to take to Hoboken. I will not charge on the exemption."

My heart crashed to the floor.

"I'm confused, Your Honor," Richard spoke up. "A moment ago you indicated you were going to charge on the exemption."

"Well, you know what? I changed my mind."

"Your Honor, Mr. Torrice clearly testified that he made a move to Mount Laurel because he had a problem paying rent and then, when he fixed that problem, he was moving back."

"What did he testify to?"

"He said he moved to Hoboken, had trouble paying rent, was moving back to Mount Laurel initially, and then was able to make the rent work and was moving back to Hoboken."

"So he was moving to Hoboken. He wasn't moving to Mount Laurel. He can't be excused for carrying the guns to Mount Laurel."

I couldn't tell if Judge Morley was just a confused old man or if he was trying to distort the truth in order to guarantee my conviction.

The jury was brought back in.

"Be seated, please. Be seated, gentlemen. All right. Ladies and gentlemen, we are now ready for closing arguments. Under New Jersey Practice each attorney has only one opportunity to address you at the end of the case, and we give the party having the burden of proof—that is the State —the last word. Mr. Gilbert, please."

"Thank you, Your Honor," Richard said as he stood up from the defense table, making his way towards the jury. "As I said to you before, Brian Aitken stands before the jury accused of possessing his own property. Now, I realize we all believe in

New Jersey's various forms of gun control, but sometimes gun control can go too far. Gun control goes too far when somebody is moving between their residences and is arrested even though the officer knows that he is moving.

Gun control also goes too far when a mother maybe calls for help because she's concerned about her son and, instead of helping the son out or taking him to the hospital to see if he needs help they go after his firearms and arrest him for owning them."

The jurors hung on every word.

"This is a case of gun control going just a little too far afield here," Richard continued. "New Jersey law does allow you to possess your guns when you're moving between residences and that is what Brian was doing.

Now, the State's gong to say that this is just an excuse, that Brian was moving for a total period of six months and this is only an excuse to carry guns around in his car. There is no evidence of this.

Brian made a discreet move of his guns from Colorado to New Jersey one time and he needed to move them one more time, and that's what he was doing.

The State takes the position that for something to be a move it has to be one discreet move from one place to another at one time.

Now, this is why we have a jury system. Because we need you to apply your common sense here in a situation like this. We've all moved and we all know that unless you hire a moving van with professional movers who come in and pack and do everything in a day, it just doesn't work that way. It takes multiple trips. It can be a difficult process. The State wants to act as though it is a single discreet movement, but that's simply not the way life works."

Gilbert then asked the jury what proof had been presented that the magazines were capable of holding more than fifteen rounds. The law requires that a high capacity magazine must be "capable of holding more than 15 rounds of ammunition to be fed continuously and directly therefrom into a semiautomatic firearm."

But they had no evidence that the magazines I had were capable of doing that. The State hadn't performed any tests. They didn't have any laboratory reports. We didn't even know if they worked. The same was said for the hollow-point ammunition. No tests were performed to see if they worked and no experts testified that the ammunition found in my car was actually hollow-point ammunition as defined, or rather not defined, by New Jersey law.

"In the criminal process, we have to prove that somebody violated the law beyond a reasonable doubt.

Regarding the handguns, we heard that Brian purchased these firearms lawfully when he lived in Colorado. He underwent a Federal background check. He underwent a State background check. He filled out all the required forms. These are not items that he went and bought from a friend of a friend, trying to do something off the books. This is all above-board. This is strictly by the law and by the book.

So now we have New Jersey saying, well, that may be all fine and good in Colorado, but you have to leave them there. That just doesn't make sense. It's obvious that if you're moving your personal possessions back, whether we like what personal possessions you have or not, they're legal to possess here. He's allowed to move them back, and when he is moving them back he is entitled to keep them in his trunk, unloaded and locked, and that's exactly how they were.

This is his legitimately purchased property, and in the end Brian, as Michael Torrice testified, did his best to comply with the laws. He actually researched the New Jersey Statutes. Michael saw it. He did his best to follow them. He did not try to break any law, and I do not believe the State can prove beyond a reasonable doubt that Brian violated any New Jersey law.

Thank you."

With that Richard concluded his closing argument. Brennan was up next, and he didn't intend on being outdone.

"Listen, with all due respect to Mr. Gilbert, a lot of things you heard him just say are not what you're going to be charged with. Your job is very important, but in this particular case what you have to do is very simple.

Mr. Aitken is not being prosecuted for owning his own property. He's being prosecuted for carrying guns around in an illegal way. You can't carry a firearm—and when you have it in your car you're carrying it—without a permit. And that's what happened here. If you read the law, Mr. Aitken is guilty of the three charges that he was indicted for.

Let me talk briefly as your tour guide here for a moment. Mr. Aitken was going through a divorce and the evidence is clear his purpose in coming to Mount Laurel that day was to pick up his mother for visitation with his son.

And this isn't a situation where the State of New Jersey is overzealous and overbearing—putting their nose into people's lives like they always do with everything else. No. His parents called the police on him. That's why the State got involved, not because it's some oppressive Communist regime or whatever. It was a safety issue: 'The kid's got three guns, he's acting out, we're calling the police'—that's why we're all here.

He's taking three guns from Hoboken and coming down to Mount Laurel. He wasn't moving anything. He had bags in his car because he was coming down to spend the weekend with his parents because of the visitation. And, how do we know that? Because when the visitation was canceled he didn't stay with his parents. He was gone.

Those are the facts.

You're not going to be charged anything on moving. Mr. Gilbert spent most of his presentation talking about moving, but there's no rational basis under the facts of this case to believe that he was moving so you're not even going to hear that. That's not even going to be charged to you because it doesn't make any sense.

There's no excuse for what he did.

Thank you."

I was pretty sure I was fucked at this point. I lent Jenna an optimistic smile. I didn't want her to know how royally screwed I thought we really were. I could tell she knew in her heart that I'd be found innocent.

It was only lunchtime, but the day had turned dark. As if on cue, thunder crashed nearby and rain hammered the courthouse. "It's like a tropical storm out there," Morley worried aloud. He was concerned it might take a while for the jury to return from lunch.

The storm grew louder.

The jury was brought in and the doors were locked behind them.

"Ladies and gentlemen, the evidence in this case has been presented and the attorneys have completed their summations. We now arrive at that time when you as jurors are to perform your final function in this case. At the outset, let me express my thanks and appreciation to you for your attention to this case. I would like to commend counsel for the professional manner in which they have presented their respective cases and for their courtesy to the Court and jury during the course of this trial.

Before you retire to deliberate and reach your verdict, it is my obligation to instruct you as to the principles of law applicable to this case. You shall consider my instructions in their entirety and not pick out any particular instruction and overemphasize it.

The State has the burden of proving the defendant guilty beyond a reasonable doubt. Some of you may have served as jurors in civil cases where you were told that it was necessary to prove only that a fact was more likely true than not true. In criminal cases, however, the State's proof must be more powerful than that. It must be beyond a reasonable doubt.

A reasonable doubt is an honest and reasonable uncertainty in your minds about the guilt of the defendant after you have given full and impartial consideration to all of the evidence.

Arguments, statements, remarks, openings and summations of counsel are not evidence and must not be treated as evidence..."

Judge Morley read the charges against me and explained what each of them meant.

"If you find that the State has failed to prove any of these elements beyond a reasonable doubt then you must return a verdict of not guilty. On the other hand, if you find that the State has proven all these elements beyond a reasonable doubt then you must return a verdict of guilty."

I caught the entire jury staring at me. They seemed hopeful. One lady smiled at me, caught herself, and tried to look more serious. Maybe I was wrong to give up my optimism so easily.

"That concludes my instructions as to the principles of law governing the offenses charged in the indictment. Very shortly you will go to the jury room to start your deliberations. You are to apply the law as I've instructed you to the facts as you find them to be for the purpose of arriving at a fair and correct verdict... and must be unanimous. All of you must agree if the defendant is guilty or not guilty on each charge.

If during your deliberations you have a question or feel that you need further assistance or instructions from me, write your question on a sheet of paper and give it to the officer who will be standing at the jury room door, who in turn will give it to me. I will then go over the question with the lawyers and I will try to answer as quickly as possible. Please be patient."

The jury was escorted out of the courtroom to begin their deliberations. I can't recall how many minutes or hours I sat there for, but it was nerve wracking. I had remembered hearing that if the jury came back too quickly it was a bad sign and that if they took too long it meant good news. Or was it the other way around? I couldn't remember.

Before I knew it the court officer returned, handing a note to the judge.

That was quick. Too quick.

"I have a question from the jury which I've had marked C-3.

> "Please define the exceptions to the law for all three charges. That is, it was announced that 'moving is an exception.' We need to be clear of all exceptions, if any, for each charge."

"Mr. Brennan, what do you think?" Morley asked of the prosecutor.

I remember feeling like the jury was smarter than the judge had anticipated. They seemed to see through his theatrics and, for a moment, I allowed myself to feel a glimmer of hope.

"Judge, there are no exceptions at this stage in this case, and I would indicate that a decision has been made that there are no exceptions to be presented. Obviously they're concerned because it was mentioned to them, but I think they're entitled to know the posture of the case at this point."

"Mr. Gilbert?"

"Your Honor, they're asking about the exemptions under New Jersey law and, respectfully, they need to be told what the exemptions are. And, it sounds like they're asking the broader question, indeed, of what other types of exemptions are out there, because they're aware that firearm ownership is legal, and they need to understand under what circumstances it is and is not legal. As I argued before, we clearly have testimony that Mr. Aitken was moving, so I think they need to hear that."

"Are you suggesting that I tell them about every exception?"

"Well, it sounds like they're asking about every exception."

"Judge, if I could?" Brennan interrupted, "The Court ruled that it wasn't going to charge the exemptions that were requested. I think you need to tell them, with all due respect to the Court, that there is no rational basis for any exceptions to be charged to this jury."

"Your Honor, there's something else, too," Richard added, "besides the moving exemption, it seems as though their question is broad enough to request the exemption for hollow-point ammunition as well. And, as we're aware, that's not illegal under all circumstances."

"It's the same exemption, right? It's legal to bring it from one legal place to another legal place as long as it's packaged the right way, correct?"

"Judge, we shouldn't even be at this point. The Court ruled..." Brennan protested.

"I just want to make sure that his position's clearly on the record," said the judge. "You're asking for the "moving" exception as to both the firearms and the hollow-points?"

"Yes, Your Honor."

"All right. But the threshold issue is whether or not he's "moving," and I've already ruled that he isn't. So I think I have to tell the jury that it's my responsibility to decide as a matter of law whether any exceptions may be considered by the jury, and I have ruled in this case that the evidence does not justify my charging them with any exceptions. Isn't that consistent with my ruling? Isn't that what I ruled?"

"That is consistent with your ruling, Your Honor," Richard conceded. But, just because someone is consistent does not necessarily make them correct.

"Ok, would you bring the jury in?" Morley asked the bailiff.

Once the sheep were shuffled in, Morley shot down their inquisition.

"I have received your note.

As the judge of the law in this case it is my responsibility in deciding what to charge you to determine whether there's a basis in the evidence for any particular charge, including whether there is a basis in the evidence for telling you about any exceptions that may apply in this case, exceptions to the requirement of having a permit to carry a firearm, to possess a firearm. I have, as a matter of law, determined that the evidence in this case does not provide a basis for me to instruct you as to any exception and, therefore, you are not to consider whether any exception applies. Does that answer your question?"

They stared blankly back at him.

"All right. If that is unclear please send me another note, try to clarify it and I'll try to make it more explicit. Okay? Short answer: I've determined that you are not to consider any exceptions in this case. All right? Thank you, folks."

The jury was sent back to deliberate and, within minutes, the court officer returned with another note.

"All right. Returning to the Aitken matter, I have a note marked C-4,

> "When can you transport a weapon in your
> car without a permit?"

"Mr. Brennan, what do you think?"

"I think the answer would be never, Judge, based on the

posture of the case."

"Mr. Gilbert?"

"Your Honor's already familiar with my arguments. I believe the jury's requesting the exemptions."

"Yeah, they are. They unquestionably are, but I've already concluded that no exceptions apply. Would you bring the jury back, please?"

One by one they were prodded back into place.

"Please be seated. I received another note from the jury, which has been marked C-4, and it reads "When can you transport a weapon in your car without a permit?" You may transport a weapon in a car without a permit only under those conditions where the law provides an exception to the requirement that you possess a permit. And as I told you a few moments ago I have determined as a matter of law that the evidence in this case does not justify my presenting to you for your consideration any of the exceptions that are listed in the Statute. All right? Thank you. Would you retire, please?"

Again, the jury was escorted out, defeated. They had come back two times practically begging the judge for the exemptions, but he didn't seem to care. He appeared to be doing anything and everything within his power to make sure I was found guilty.

It was becoming clear to me that my case never had anything to do with right and wrong and it sure as hell never had anything to do with the law. This was political and the State wanted nothing more than to make an example out of me— to let the entire country know they don't care what the law says or doesn't say: if you step foot in New Jersey with a gun, you're going to jail.

With that, we broke for the night. It was a rough day, and Kristen—Jenna's best friend—drove the two of us back up to New York, battle-worn from another full day of attacks.

The next morning the jury confronted the judge with a final, defiant, show of resistance.

"I received a note from the jury," Judge Morley said, "It has been marked as Exhibit C-6.

> "Why did you make us aware at the start of the trial that the law allows a person to carry a weapon if the person is moving or going to a shooting range, and during the trial both the defense and prosecution presented testimony as to whether or not the defendant was in the process of moving, and then in your charge for us to deliberate we are not permitted to take into consideration whether or not we believe the defendant was moving?"

"Mr. Brennan?"

"Well, Judge, obviously we have a perceptive group. I don't

know how many times you have to tell them, but I think you have to tell them even more sternly that you've told them twice, and now you're telling them a third time that what you say is the law."

"Well, I would note that I did not say anything at the start of the trial about moving or shooting range or anything like that."

"Well, I think you need to tell them that the defense affirmatively pled these things. And you've ruled, as a matter of law, that there's not a rational basis to charge the jury with the exceptions."

"Mr. Gilbert?"

"Judge, again, I'm objecting," Richard said. "Please tell them the law. There is evidence to support it. We clearly have three witnesses to support it, and it should have been told to them. They need to understand the entire law to come to a proper resolution of this case. They deserve to know the law.

Your Honor, coming into this trial I had every indication and every understanding that you would be charging at least the New Jersey charge."

"That's why we have a charge conference. I think the suggestion is that I misled you. I didn't mislead you. I expressed no opinion. I knew from our various conferences that was an approach you intended to take and I didn't inhibit you in any way from advancing what evidence and testimony you may have on the issue. You might argue otherwise, because I didn't let you bring in the closing documents, but I didn't mislead anybody here about what I was going to charge.

I don't—I don't—that's not the way I operate. That's not the way I'm supposed to operate," Judge Morley stammered, "I wait until I hear all of the evidence in the case and then I make a decision on what my charge is going to be. Would you bring the jury in, please?"

"Yes, sir." The young clerk obliged.

The judge lowered his glasses and began to lecture the jury. I'd seen third graders given more respect.

"Let me emphasize to you I did not tell you that the law allows a person to carry a weapon when he is moving or going to a shooting range. I did not do that.

As I've already told you, based on all of the evidence in the case I have ruled as a matter of law that the defendant is not entitled to have you consider whether he is entitled to an exemption to the permit requirement based on his argument that he was moving. That is a legal determination, which is for me to make. I decide what charges go to the jury. I decide what defenses go to the jury, and I make those purely for legal reasons.

The issue of whether the defendant was in the process of moving and, therefore, entitled to an exemption to the permit requirement is not before you. Thank you, ladies and gentlemen. If you would retire, please, and continue your deliberations."

What I heard sounded more like this, "Listen, I keep telling you to find him guilty and you keep coming back to me asking about these silly laws. I AM THE LAW. Now, go back there and find him guilty so we can all go home. All right? Thank you."

I wasn't sure what the jury was going to do. It was clear to me they wanted the exemptions, but the judge was forcing them into a corner; forcing them to convict me. There was a chance they could ignore the judge's charges completely and find me not guilty. The practice is called Jury Nullification. It's a little known secret that defense lawyers are prohibited from telling the jury about it.

Jury Nullification is when a jury acquits a criminal defendant who is technically guilty, but who the jury does not feel deserves to be punished. The jury reaches a verdict that contradicts the judge's instructions. Most jurors don't know this is even an option and, despite our freedom of speech, supporters of nullification have been thrown in prison for handing out educational pamphlets in front of courthouses.

It's one of the most sacred constitutional doctrines we have: the ability to find a law unjust and to vote with our conscience. But it challenges the authority of judges, and most are not fans of having their authority challenged. Our founding fathers understood the importance of this doctrine and even John Adams once said, "It is not only [the juror's] right, but his duty...to find the verdict according to his own best understanding, judgment, and conscience, though in direct opposition to the direction of the court."

Likewise, John Jay, the first chief justice of the Supreme Court, said, "The jury has the right to judge both the law as well as the fact in controversy."

The need for jurors to be educated about their right to nullify had recently been heard by the Ninth Circuit Court of Appeals.

In February of 2003, a California jury convicted marijuana activist Ed Rosenthal of growing marijuana, in violation of federal law.

What the jury didn't know — and wasn't allowed to hear — was that Rosenthal was not only growing the marijuana for medical patients, but he was also commissioned by the city of Oakland to grow the stuff. After the trial, the jury was outraged. "'I'm sorry' doesn't begin to cover it," one juror told *The New York Times*.

"It's the most horrible mistake I've ever made in my entire life," the jury foreman added.

The phrase above, "wasn't allowed to hear," resonated loudly with my case.

The jury knew something was rotten in Denmark. I could see it in their eyes. They were being bullied. They were being told "find that boy guilty, or else." But, there was still hope they could find me innocent and nullify the charges.

The court officer came back with a final note from the jury and handed it to the judge.

"I have received a note from the jury that reads 'We have arrived at a verdict.'—Would you bring the jury in, please?"

Their once friendly faces now refused to make eye contact with me. They stared at the floor in front of them, afraid they might catch a glimpse of the man they were about to condemn.

They didn't need to say a word—their looks of shame said it all.

CHAPTER NINE

We had everything we needed to win, and we had come so close, but without the jury being allowed to consider the statutory exceptions I was screwed. Morley knew that and whatever grudge he held against me for appearing on FOX manifested itself when he did the jury's job for them.

There was a two-month period between being found guilty and actually being sentenced and walking into prison. The prosecutor tried to peg me as a flight-risk and have me incarcerated immediately until sentencing, but I surrendered my passport and the judge agreed to let me out on bail until my sentencing in August. It probably didn't hurt that they still had the $10,000 bail my dad had given them eighteen months earlier.

On June 17th, just two weeks after my trial was heard,

Governor Christie announced he wasn't appointing Judge Morley to his life term on the bench. Effective immediately, he was no longer a sitting judge.

Talk about shitty timing.

Morley's name was hitting all the major newspapers.

The Philadelphia Daily News wrote "A Burlington County Superior Court judge who has raised eyebrows and drawn national headlines for his comments from the bench may soon be looking for another job."

Apparently, I wasn't the only person who'd been left unsatisfied.

The governor gave no official reason for excluding Morley from the list of sitting judges reappointed to the bench, but he didn't need to. Morley's decisions spoke for themselves.

During a grand jury proceeding over which he presided, Judge Morley dismissed animal cruelty charges filed against a Moorestown, New Jersey police officer accused of having sexual relations with calves. Morley argued that the grand jury could not determine if the calves, which were shown on video giving the police officer oral sex, were "tormented" or "puzzled" by the actions.

"If the cow had the cognitive ability to form thought and speak, would it say, 'Where's the milk? I'm not getting any milk,' " Judge Morley said during the grand jury proceeding.

"Children enjoy the act of suckling," the judge said. "Cows may be of a different disposition." The judge's logic was simple: it's not animal abuse because you can't prove the cows didn't enjoy it.

Shortly afterward, that police officer, Robert Melia, was charged with forty-one crimes related to molesting three underage girls. He was convicted of twenty-two of the charges including first-degree aggravated sexual assault, child endangerment, and official misconduct.

The prosecutor, Kevin Morgan, called Melia's bestiality "a crime against nature," adding that "any reasonable juror" could infer that the act was torment. Morley said the question before him was not a question of morality or hygiene, but of the law. Bestiality is not against the law in New Jersey.

In a second and equally disturbing case, Judge Morley ruled that a forty-five-year-old teacher's aide was not a predator for having sex with a sixteen-year-old-old boy, pointing out that had the woman not been a teacher's aide, her actions would not have even been a crime since the age of consent in New Jersey is sixteen. He casually ignored the massive amount of trust parents place in schools, and teachers, to not molest their children.

When Governor Christie decided the people of New Jersey had probably seen enough of Judge James Morley, I was given a few extra weeks of relative freedom while a replacement judge was found to take over his caseload. There was some comfort in knowing that Morley wouldn't be the judge deciding how many years I'd spend behind bars.

After I was found guilty, a reporter's query prompted the Burlington County Prosecutor's office to respond, "There was no evidence produced at the trial by the defendant that warranted such a defense."

Morley told FoxNews.com that his recollection of the trial record "did not establish that [Aitken] was in the process of moving." When asked to elaborate he declined.

He later told a reporter that the testimony about me moving "was irrelevant," which followed the same distorted logic that the prosecutor's office had used. "There was no evidence that Mr. Aitken was moving. He was trying to argue that the law should give him this broad window extending over several weeks to justify driving around with guns in his car," Morley said. But no one ever testified that I was driving around for weeks at a time with the guns in my car. That was just something Morley made up.

My lawyers didn't hold back when journalists called their offices. What did they have to lose? It wasn't like Morley was even a judge anymore, so they wouldn't have to worry about him presiding over one of their cases in the future. Besides, I was already on my way towards spending the better part of a decade behind bars.

"New Jersey gun laws are insane," Evan Nappen—one of my lawyers—told reporters. "It makes a criminal of every gun owner and forces him to prove his innocence."

"There's a wide patchwork of gun laws between various jurisdictions, and in some states, it can differ from a local town that passes an ordinance to another town," he told Joshua Miller of FOX News.

Nappen explained that it wasn't even Morley's job to decide whether I was moving. "That's a question of fact, not law, and questions of fact are supposed to be determined by the jury," he said. "The judge is supposed to instruct the jury on the law, and in this case, he refused to let them even hear it. But besides that, for him to say there was no evidence presented that Brian was moving just isn't true."

He wasn't just griping to the media about how unfair my trial had been. In the background Nappen and Gilbert were hard at work preparing a motion to release me on bail pending appeal. My lawyers were confident that the convictions would be overturned on appeal and thought it would be unjust for me to be incarcerated during the lengthy appeals process.

Jenna was especially optimistic that I'd be free while the Appellate Division heard my appeal. I didn't have the heart to tell her that was never going to happen. I'd seen enough of this court's brand of justice to know better.

We weren't the only ones having a hard time accepting my new Orwellian reality. My father was at a complete loss for words when he was interviewed by FOX News, "I don't think there are words yet invented that could characterize the —I guess anger would be one word, but it's a lot deeper than anger," he said. "Whatever the word is that's a combination of anger, shock, disbelief, horror and a desire to expose all of this—that's the word. This can't happen. I won't let this happen to my son."

By then, Jenna and I had gotten rid of our lease on our loft in Hoboken and were living at her parents' house in Orange County, New York. With the guilty verdict in, we knew I'd be going to jail, but the question remained: for how long? Jenna and I spent every day together, waiting for the inevitable; for some new stranger to decide my fate, again.

Jenna was a pro when it came to hiding her vulnerability, but with the walls crashing down around us she couldn't help but wear her heart on her sleeve.

"I don't know what I'm going to do," she buried her head in my chest and dug her fingers into my arms, "I'm not as strong as you are. I'm not strong enough for this."

I could feel her tears slowly soaking through my t-shirt while we lay in bed, with my dog curled up at our feet. I didn't know what to tell her. The truth seemed too hard; too unreal. Too demanding of an innocent girl like her.

"I know," I whispered, "It's going to be ok," I said, wanting desperately to believe my own lie.

I was sentenced on August 27, 2010 in the same Burlington County courtroom that my trial had been held. Since Morley had been more-or-less kicked off the bench I had a different judge preside over my sentencing. It was this judge's first time sentencing in criminal court—he was brought in temporarily from the family division. I thought that would give me a clean slate to work with while we asked for leniency in the sentence and to let me out on bail pending the outcome of my appeals.

I was wrong.

Morley had made sure the new judge knew his position, and had even made a sentencing recommendation in the case notes he left behind. There were a number of mitigating factors for the new judge to consider that could have allowed him to ease up on the sentence, which had a range of five to ten years with a mandatory minimum of three years in prison before becoming eligible for parole. On the one hand, I had never committed a crime before, was unlikely to commit any crimes in the future, going to prison for five to ten years would be an excessive punishment, and I would be a good candidate for probation.

At the center of all of this was one glaring fact: I hadn't hurt a single person, and had no intent to commit any crime whatsoever.

Despite those facts, the judge had his marching orders from Morley—still carelessly destroying lives from beyond the bench—not to mention the directive from the Attorney General that told the State to make an example out of gun-owners.

"I'm going to deny the motion. The rule provides that a defendant in a criminal action shall be submitted to bail on motion only if it appears that the case involves a substantial question that should be determined by the Appellate Court, and you have to meet all of these; that the safety of any person or of the community will not be seriously threatened if the defendant remains on bail and that there is no significant risk of defendant's flight.

Here, I don't find that the defendant has established that there are any substantial issues that need to be determined by the Appellate Division... obviously I wasn't here at the trial, and folks haven't given me the transcript to review, but I don't think you could have the weapon in your car continuously and then say 'I'm moving'... I just don't see an Appellate court reviewing this. I have to go with what the folks are telling me here. But, in terms of whether there's a substantial question that should be determined by the Appellate Division, I just can't find that there is."

The writing was on the wall. This judge only knew what the prosecutor and judge had told him about my case and didn't even think an Appellate court would look at my case. With my motion for bail denied I braced myself for the worst.

"Okay," the judge looked over at Brennan, "can we proceed with sentencing?"

"Yes, Judge," Brennan explained how I'd been convicted of all three charges, the most serious of which was recently upgraded to a Second Degree felony thanks to the Graves Act, which made possession of a firearm the same level offense as using a firearm to commit a violent crime.

"I think someone reading this presentence report can obviously reach the conclusion that Mr. Aitken was taking a handgun from Hoboken to his court-ordered supervised visitation with his son in Toms River Township. I don't think that's an unfair inference."

I couldn't believe what I was hearing.

No witness had ever even suggested that this was a possibility, and now the prosecutor was trying to pass this off as a reasonable conclusion to a judge who hadn't heard a single word of testimony. Brennan's intention appeared clear: he was trying to present me as having nefarious intentions. According to Brennan, I probably could have shot and killed my own son. The possibilities were endless.

Brennan was a special kind of scoundrel.

"THAT'S NOT TRUE!" I heard my mother cry out.

"Ma'am, ma'am, if you say something else I'm going to have to ask you to leave. Go ahead, Mr. Brennan. Continue."

"Thank you, Judge. I'm arguing that the defendant should be sentenced to seven years, three years mandatory minimum."

"Thank you," the judge said looking over at Richard, "Counsel?"

"Good morning, Your Honor. I disagree with a lot of the factual contentions within the presentence report and, for the record, I do not stipulate to any of the facts. Mr. Aitken has never been in serious trouble. He's been a law-abiding citizen. He is a businessman. He wants to establish and grow his business and, therefore, is not likely to commit another offense.

What we have here is a young father, a responsible gentleman who has—according to New Jersey's law—made one mistake.

I believe imprisonment would be an excessive hardship. Not only is it disproportionate to what I believe occurred here, but also it will essentially end his company, put twelve people out of work, and cause great hardship. He will no longer be able to support his young son and will probably lose custody or any parenting time that he wishes with his son.

I'm aware the Graves Act requires a certain minimum sentence; under other circumstances I would be here arguing for straight probation. Given these circumstances I would simply request that you provide Mr. Aitken with the minimum that you're allowed to provide."

"Thank you very much, sir," the judge said turning his attention to the microphone, "In terms of count one I find the following aggravating and mitigating factors. I don't think there's any risk he'll commit another offense. But I do find a strong need for deterring the defendant and others from violating the law so that the public is aware that there are penalties for offenses of this type."

In other words, he knew I was not a criminal but wanted to sentence me harshly just to make an example out of me to other gun owners across the country. The message was clear: move here with your guns, legal or not, and you'll regret it.

"On count one of indictment number 09-03-002171, I sentence the defendant to seven years in New Jersey State Prison..."

The room went black and the volume turned off. Nothing else he had to say mattered.

Seven years. Seven. Fucking. Years.

CHAPTER TEN

I'm sure that wherever Judge Morley was enjoying his mandatory early retirement, he was bathing in the satisfaction that he'd gotten the last word with that insolent boy and his guns. But, I've never been a good loser—and I wasn't about to roll over now.

If anything, Morley and Brennan's shameless disregard for the truth renewed my resolve to fight and I vowed to myself that I'd be out on appeal soon, maybe only two or three years down the road. It didn't matter how long it would take, time was all I had now.

With my sentencing reached, Jenna burst through the gate separating spectators from the lawyers and threw her arms around my neck, squeezing me tightly before the bailiff gently grabbed her by the arm and guided her back to the gallery. There was no time for goodbyes—I was going directly from sentencing to jail. It would be a long time before I'd be allowed to hug her again for any longer than a brief moment.

Before being taken away, I handed Richard the Swiss watch I'd been wearing, "Make sure Jenna gets this," I told him, "It'll pay for the appeal."

As I was escorted into the back of the Burlington County Detention Center, I consoled myself with the fact that I had great lawyers, and an amazing family, who wouldn't stop fighting for me. Richard and I had already discussed the appeal and, to my novice eyes, it seemed solid and practically irrefutable.

The appeal was made of five prongs. First, we argued that the judge was incorrect when he failed to provide the jury instructions on the state and federal exemptions for the lawful possession of firearms and ammunition.

Point two said that the court erred by failing to dismiss the unlawful possession charge against me because the prosecutor's office had failed to provide enough substantial information on those exemptions to the grand jury. In other words, if the prosecutor had explained the exemptions to the grand jury, I probably never would have been charged and there never would have been a trial. The whole thing could have been thrown out before it even started if the prosecution had just been open and honest with the grand jury.

Points three and four of the appeal argued that New Jersey's ban on standard-capacity magazines—which New Jersey referred to as "high-capacity magazines"—was unconstitutional and that the evidence used against me during the grand jury proceedings should never have been permitted since the very nature of the search of my car in my parents' driveway was itself illegal. The Mount Laurel cops simply had no right to even ask me to consent to a search, let alone actually conduct the search.

And finally, we stressed that the second amendment protected my ownership of the pistols and the ammunition.

As I left the courtroom, I was taken through the back room where the guards initially mistook me for a lawyer, before riding the elevator down to a basement corridor and into what they euphemistically called "processing." The multistory U-shaped detention center is part of a one-acre complex in which trials are held, sentences rendered, and new prisoners are locked up while they await either bail or, in my case, assignments to bigger and more permanent prisons. The Burlington County Detention Center was a purgatory for the convicted and the poor. It was a mix of dirt and ugliness and potentially lethal conversations—a place where the wrong look or the wrong comment at the wrong time could provoke serious repercussions.

To the uninitiated, the concept of a "jail" seems almost

benign. They are not. Jails are harsh, dirty, unfriendly, cold, bare and devoid of community. They are temporary warehouses for prisoners waiting to go somewhere else. In many ways, a county jail is more dangerous than prison. With their ecru-cinderblock walls, horrible food, and mandatory conformity, jail reminded me of public school.

There is no time for a new prisoner to absorb whatever rules there are. There is no place to hide. No cliques to protect you, other than ones you might find by accident or initiation —neither of which do the innocent any good. You either sink or swim. I kept my head up and my mouth shut. I learned from watching other newbies, but it was only a matter of time before they got to you.

Posers are quickly discovered, and can be humiliated in all sorts of ways, from mere ridicule to being beaten with a padlock stuffed in a tube sock. By the time he makes it back from the infirmary, he's no longer a poser. He's either broken or hardened.

Jails are really just massive storage units for discarded and unwanted souls waiting for a permanent home. Usually these inmates have sentences of less than a year. Some are awaiting trial and can't make bail. Some have just been thrown into the mix for a day or two. These guys included the drunk drivers who hadn't sobered up enough to get a lawyer and the idiots who failed to make a required court appearance and were hauled in for a warrant after being stopped for a minor traffic infraction.

The new inmate is in "population" with everyone. The guy who got too drunk with his buddies the night before might find himself next to a pedophile or murderer. That's just how jails are. And because prisoners in jail are temporary, the correction officers who guard them can be as vicious and brutal as they chose to be. There is no institutional memory in jails, no chance for a prisoner who had the shit beaten out of him by a guard to somehow avenge himself later. I soon got the impression that many C.O.'s, as they called the corrections officers, were guys who had failed the entrance exams for their local police force and turned to this as a way to get to wear a uniform and order people around without fear of reprisal.

Prisons, by contrast, are in their own weird way more organized and safe. There are established rules, social hierarchies, and long-term memories. That is not to say that prisons are in any way pleasant places to be, but in the skewed world of incarceration, they are preferred to jails.

It didn't take long to learn that there were two sets of rules; the official rules of conduct issued by the jail and the unofficial guidelines of survival that you learn from experience. And for the second—and by far the most important—set of rules you had better be a quick study. I thought I'd be fine just keeping my head low and staying off the radar, but I was wrong.

The official rules enforced by the C.O.'s and the warden were pretty straightforward. They told you how to stand in line; how to use the bathroom; how to make your bed; what to do during "count", and; to hit the floor and show your hands if the alarms began to sound.

The unofficial rules, the rules set up by the prisoners themselves, were the ones you really had to pay attention to. Practically everyone I was in jail with had been there before. They knew the rules, and they enforced the rules, and the rules changed to suit whoever was running things. For some of these guys, being in jail was a vacation from the real danger of the ghetto. Jail allowed them a little peace and an opportunity to recharge before hitting the streets again. These were the guys who commanded an unusual hybrid of fear and respect, and I learned very quickly who they were.

After my first night, I woke to the sound of the Muslim morning prayer—the *Fajr* Prayer—something I would hear every morning I was there. It was the first of five prayer sessions that devout Muslims were required to make. I'd never heard it before. Something about it was both beautiful and mesmerizing.

From my cell above, I heard a couple dozen men on the ground floor below reciting the prayer. Through the bars, I could just barely make out some of them standing or kneeling on rugs facing the Muslim Holy city of Mecca, holding their hands up to their ears. The words "Allah

Akbar" shouted in unison by dozens of men was clear: "God is Great." Men find religion in prison, though I questioned how sincere their religious intent was. As I got to know them, I realized these were not exactly petty thieves, but hardcore criminals and repeat offenders. Rapists. Murderers. Drug lords. Those were the types of guys who were praying. I suppose they needed redemption more than anyone else.

Most of these devout men were gang members—almost exclusively Bloods. In New Jersey, the Bloods are one of the more prominent gangs among minorities, and many Bloods were loyal Muslims. One morning, a young Blood stopped at my cell on his way back from morning prayer.

"Yo," the young Blood said in a loud whisper peering through the bars of my cell. I looked around but my albino roommate wasn't there.

"Yes?" I replied, wondering what he wanted.

"You ordered commissary, right"

"Yes, why?"

"You gotta give me three packets."

He looked at me intensely.

"What? Why would I do that?" I didn't have any idea what he meant. Three packets of what?

"Three packets. What the fuck's your problem? Three packets a week. Fuck, man," he said as he grew irritated, "Three fucking packets." And he walked away. Clearly, I was missing something.

My cellmate returned a little while later and I told him what had happened. He was a tall skinny albino with red hair and freckles who said he was "blacker than most of these pussy motherfuckers" in here. According to him, he was well known in Camden as one of the bigger drug dealers in the most dangerous city in America.

"Those mothafuckas don't know who the fuck they're fuckin' with," he said after I explained what had happened. Those were Bloods, and they were extorting the cell—extorting me—for protection. The packets he demanded as payment were packets of food, usually mackerel or tuna—chicken if you really had money.

"Don't you give them a fuckin' thing. No one from this cell is giving them shit. That young buck doesn't even fucking know." My cellmate was pissed.

Somehow, my cellmate convinced the guards to let him out and he wandered down to the cell of an older inmate, probably in his thirties. This guy was also a Blood, allegedly in for murder and waiting on bail that would never come. I could hear my cellmate yelling at him from thirty yards away.

"You don't have to worry about those niggas," he said to me

when he came back.

"They didn't know who the fuck you were bunkin' with." He paused, looked me up and down before meeting my stare. "You can't give these motherfuckers an inch, man. You're new. You don't know this shit. But you gotta know. They wanna see how much they can get outta you. First it's three packets. Then it's four. Then it's what fucking ever. You gotta stop that shit before it starts."

He was emphatic, "Them young bucks don't know me, but their boy fuckin' knows who I am, and you ain't gotta worry about that shit while I'm here."

Then he sat down at the single metal desk in our cell, painted khaki and bolted to the concrete khaki wall, and pulled out a deck of cards to play solitaire.

This was my life now.

Halfway into his game, the albino asked me, "What'd you do?"

"I'd rather not talk about it."

"You're not a fucking pedophile are you? Fuck. Don't tell me I just stuck my neck out for no fucking pedophile."

"What? No." What the hell was this guy talking about now? Did I look like a pedophile? I didn't even know what a pedophile looked like.

"Only pedophiles don't tell people what they're in for man, otherwise there ain't nothin' to hide in here. We're all gonna find out eventually, anyway, man."

"Guns."

"Guns?" he rolled a cigarette with some loose tobacco. "No, man, no. Ain't no fucking way. What'd you really do?"

"Illegal possession of guns, hollowpoints, and high-capacity magazines." I said, looking up from my orange government-issued slippers.

"My nigga! You white boys always got the fuckin' arsenals! Who were you moving for?"

"I wasn't selling them, I was just moving them from my parents' house to my apartment."

"Nooooooo. No, no, no, man. You was doing something, otherwise you wouldn't be holed up in here. You was up to something. They were hot weren't they?"

He ashed his cigarette in the stainless steel toilet.

"No, they were mine."

I tried to tell him as little as possible but, eventually, wound up telling him everything.

"No. Fucking. Way. Shit, man, are you telling me of all the motherfuckers in here who say their innocent I got bunked up with the one motherfucker who really is?"

I looked at him, unsure what to say. Everyone in prison claims they're innocent, right?

This conversation in one form or another would repeat itself numerous times with every new person who was introduced to me. It got to the point when people asked me what I "was in for" I would just look away and not answer them. I got sick of explaining it. The people around me knew the story well enough and they'd do the talking for me.

"You done pissed someone off, man. Did you piss off the judge or something?"

I looked around at the graffiti scratched into the paint on all four walls around me. People's names had been scratched into anything with a painted surface. The steel bunk frame, the walls, the desk. Months and years were scratched into every surface.

I laid my head down on my pillow.

"You have no idea."

+++

The schedule in jail was what they called "23+1"—twenty-three hours spent indoors and one hour a day outside in the "yard" for recreation. The entire twenty-three hours didn't need to be spent in our cell. We had a small amount of time to eat meals in the mess hall and could spend a couple of hours in a common area, where inmates mostly sat at tables to play chess, watch TV, or wait in line to use the payphones.

Lunch and dinner was usually a cold hot dog with a stale slice of white bread and baked beans. Breakfast gruel was optimistically called oatmeal. Meals were usually limited to ten minutes, and many of the veterans could inhale a dinner in less than sixty seconds. My dinner neighbors waited anxiously to see what I wouldn't eat, which for the first four days was everything.

Inmates came and went. At times, the overcrowding was so bad that people had to sleep on plastic sleds. The sleds had a thin mattress pad, no more than two inches thick, and were kept beneath the bunk during the day. At night, an unlucky inmate would pull the sled out in front of the toilet—the only place with enough space that the sled could fit—and hope none of his cellies would have to piss, or worse, in the middle of the night. Some cells had two or three sleds in them, meaning a room intended to house two people had as many as five or six inmates in them. The conditions quickly became uncontrollably filthy. The overcrowding made me wonder if New Jersey had fallen victim to an obscene influx of criminal activity or if its citizens were victims of an out-of-control prison industrial complex.

With recent headlines in Rolling Stone blaring "School-to-Prison Pipeline: A Nationwide Problem for Equal Rights" and ABC's "Pennsylvania Judge Convicted in 'Kids for Cash' Scheme" it was obvious judges and prosecutors all across the country had less-than-honorable motivators for sending people to jail. Students were being thrown in prison for dress-code violations and talking back to teachers. Coupled with the insane number of people whose only crimes were possession of a harmless plant, it was no surprise people were practically sleeping on top of each other.

I spent most of my time outside of the cell waiting to use the payphones. I called Jenna every chance I could get, and the cost was exorbitant. Someone is making a fortune off their monopoly servicing collect-calls from inmates to their loved ones.

I was allowed non-contact booth visits behind-Plexiglas on Wednesdays, and contact-visits in the gymnasium on Saturdays. Even though it took her eight hours roundtrip to visit, Jenna came every single week, just to see me for an hour.

Jenna's first visit was awkward, painful, and short.

"Aitken, get your ass down here, you've got a visitor!" I buttoned up my orange jumpsuit with the bold letters "BCDC" screen-printed on the back—in case there was any question who I belonged to—and stood for inspection at the gate to my cell.

"All right," the corrections officer said looking me up and

down, "let's go."

I wasn't sure what to expect. I couldn't wait to see her and hug her, even if it had only been a week since I was sentenced. Every time I passed through a steel gate, I felt one step closer to holding her again. I've never needed anyone as much as I needed Jenna in those months, but I veiled my emotions with a determination to break free. I used every emotion—longing, loneliness, fear, anger—to fuel my desire to fight. When I walked into the visitation room, I saw the plexiglass wall partitioning visitors from inmates and realized, at best, all I could do was touch my fingertips to hers with an inch of bulletproof glass keeping us from feeling the warmth of the other.

I sat down in my plastic chair and saw her father sitting across from me, next to my Jenna, and we each picked up a black phone receiver.

"Hello, Brian," I heard the faint British accent of Jenna's father, as he greeted me solemnly.

"Hello, Neil."

I can't imagine this is what he had in mind for his daughter when he and his wife enthusiastically called Jenna from that party in High Falls and told her about the boy she absolutely had to meet. We sat in silence, wasting the seconds we'd all been waiting for, filling the air with whatever you're supposed to say to your girlfriend's father while he escorts her to see you in jail. My father used to always tell me, "You are who you surround yourself with," and I hated the thought of being lumped in with the other people dressed in orange. We weren't the same.

"Ok, then, why don't I give the two of you some privacy," Jenna's father said, taking a seat in the corner of the room and handing Jenna the receiver.

I looked through the plexiglass and saw the concern on Jenna's angelic face. I felt pure, unadulterated rage at the thought of the incestuous corruption of the prosecutor and judge. The longer I sat there the more I realized the real criminal—Judge James Morley—was the one who belonged in the flimsy plastic chair looking at his loved ones through his gold-rimmed glasses.

I unfolded a piece of paper I had hidden in my jumpsuit, flattened it out on the bench in front of me, and held it up against the plexiglass. It was a poem I'd written for her. I watched her memorize it silently, quickly, and picked up the payphone to say goodbye before we realized neither of us had words left to say.

"Do I seem different?" I asked.

"You're still you," she said. "Don't worry. And I'm still me."

I watched as they called her away and, before I knew it, I was being thoroughly strip searched—as if contraband could be passed through solid glass—before heading back up to my cell.

+++

The showers were at the end of each tier and weren't the big communal showers you see on TV. They were single-person stalls with old stained and torn plastic sheeting for privacy. They were incubators for all sorts of vile, disease-causing parasites.

One of the most dangerous bugs that made its way around jail was methicillin-resistant *Staphylococcus aureus* (MRSA), which has been emerging as a threat to public health in recent years, especially in correctional settings. Outbreaks have been seen in jails and prisons in Mississippi, California, Texas, and Georgia in recent years—and in New Jersey.

In 2001, an inmate successfully sued the Cumberland County freeholds for costs associated with a MRSA infection contracted in the county jail. MRSA is frequently caused by skin contact of any kind. In jail that could mean touching someone's towel, bumping up against a shower stall wall, borrowing a shirt or even shaking hands.

The inmate, James Parker, contracted a MRSA infection that led to a softball-sized boil to form on his inner thigh, which required surgery to remove in late 2007.

In his suit, Parker accused both the Cumberland County

Department of Corrections as well as the county itself of negligence for "failure to provide appropriate and proper medical treatment." He won a $125,000 settlement and pointed to the jail's overcrowding as a huge contributing factor.

"(The jail) doesn't have enough room for all the inmates," said Parker in December 2007. "You've got inmates sleeping on the floor. They treat us like animals... in a cage."

MRSA can kill, and the conditions at the Burlington County Detention Center were very much the same as Cumberland, a neighboring county to the south.

In recent years the jails reputation has gotten even worse. When you trade in your name for a number the assumption is that every inmate is the scum of the earth. But some people are in there for unpaid parking tickets, possession of marijuana, or mental illness.

One man, Robert Taylor, was a seventy-five year old homeless alcoholic who died at the Burlington County Detention Center in December of 2013. He died strapped in a "turtle suit" and lying in a pool of urine and feces, according to an anonymous supervisor inside the facility.

That same supervisor told a reporter for *The Trentonian*: "I was there when Taylor came in, and he looked really bad. A couple of us told the medical staff that he needed to go to the hospital because he was detoxing."

But Taylor was not taken to the hospital.

"We try real hard not to put anyone in the clinic if we don't have to, because it takes a C.O. off the floor," the source said.

Instead of being given any medical assistance, Taylor was placed in segregation, where he laid on the floor for five days without ever eating a single bite of food or taking a shower. An inmate in an adjacent cell said Taylor was stripped out of his clothes, strapped in an anti-suicide smock—which inmates dubbed a "turtle suit"—and then placed on suicide watch in a single-person cell with no mattress or blanket.

The inmate could smell Taylor dying, "I could smell Mr. Taylor rotting, I could smell the feces, and the urination; it was unbearable."

In an investigation the Burlington County Prosecutor, Robert Bernardi—the same prosecutor who pursued my indictment—cleared the jail of any wrongdoing. Bernardi's position seemed clear: "Inmates don't have rights and, with everything my office has to investigate, what's another dead criminal in the grand scheme of things?"

The problem is that not everyone in jail is a criminal and not all criminals deserve a death sentence.

Robert Taylor had problems and needed help. He was homeless and an alcoholic who was arrested and died, tied up, abandoned, and covered in his own feces all because he failed to pay a ninety-six dollar ticket.

He did not deserve to die.

+++

"You have a collect call from an inmate at the Burlington County Detention Center. To accept this call from BRIAN AITKEN please press one. To reject this call, please hang up."

"Hello, Brian," I heard Arden's voice—the sweet lady who always answered the phone whenever I called my lawyers.

"Hi, Arden. How are you?"

"I'm doing well. Let me get Richard for you," she said placing me on hold.

"Hello Brian, Richard here, how can I help you?"

"I was just wondering what's happening with the appeal. Is there anything I need to do? When do you think it'll be heard?"

"Well, Brian, a few things about that. First, you should know that judges don't like to rule against other judges. An appeal is a difficult thing to win. We believe we have a strong appeal, but you just never know. Now, regarding how long it could take, we should hear back from them within six months."

I had never thought about that before. It never occurred to me that an appeal was a request to a panel of judges to overturn one of their peer's decisions. When I thought about it that way I didn't feel as confident as I wanted to.

"Thanks, Richard."

"Sure thing, Brian. Anything else?"

"No, that was it."

"Ok, hang in there. We're doing our best out here for you."

"I know, Richard, thanks," I said, hanging up the phone.

I had to trust my lawyers. It was in their hands now.

CHAPTER ELEVEN

Two weeks after my first night in the county jail I was loaded into the back of a Ford Econoline van, handcuffed with my feet shackled to the floor, and transported to another temporary holding compound: the New Jersey Central Reception and Assignment Facility (CRAF).

That brief drive to Trenton was one of the only times I felt life moving ahead outside the razor wired walls of prison.

After two weeks at the Burlington County Detention Center, I had lost track of time, and I had no idea whether the trip to CRAF took thirty minute or three hours—and I wouldn't have known the difference even if I still had the watch I gave to Jenna to pawn for the cost of the appeal. I couldn't see outside the van that took us there anyway, so I had no point of reference. I could only see the faces of the other guys in there with me and the chains that held my ankles together, padlocked to the floor. I was glad to finally be leaving the jail, though. In my mind, the move symbolized progress of some sort, which is how I had dealt with everything from the beginning. Just get it over with and move on.

I never expected that I would actually miss the detention center once I was inside CRAF, which proved nothing more than a processing center for the discarded and unnamed that should have been condemned years ago.

If County Jail was Dante's first circle of the *Inferno* then Central Reception was his shit-stained third circle of hell. All hope had been abandoned by those who entered.

My own personal reception began after the cops opened up the back door of the van that had carried us from Burlington and ordered us out, one by one, to our new home filled with brick walls, concrete stairs, and short tempers. I had a very quick chance to look out toward the road that led to places where my friends had already moved on with their lives—but I couldn't see past the rows of razor wire separating me from them.

Still shackled, I took quick short steps up the concrete stairs and inside the prison to find dozens more convicts, tattooed and bald, waiting to be processed. I didn't expect a crowd.

"Hey, asshole!"

"Me?" I asked, looking up at the set of eyes between the high and tight haircut.

"Yeah, you. Clothes off."

A half dozen of us stripped off our clothes and stood naked in front of the brick wall while the guards stared at us.

"Lift 'em up, boys."

The guards eyed the colorful array of scrotums in front of them. We stood there, a rainbow of flesh, while they searched us with their eyes for contraband. Moments later, I stood in stunned silence as I saw that among the contraband pulled from various rectums along the line were several fairly large cell phones and drug-filled balloons. My education continued, and I made a mental note not to borrow any phones while I was in there.

Before I was marched inside, I looked around at the dilapidated building before me. It was an eyesore, even against the already gray and exhausted Trenton landscape. The facility was a chancre that stood out in its ugliness. But its physical appearance, as bad as it was, was nothing compared to the things that went on inside. That first body-cavity search was only the beginning.

I was told this place opened in the early 1930s as a home for the criminally insane, but there was a cornerstone in the building that dated back to 1901. It looked like Shawshank, but with a centuries worth of additional neglect.

Central Reception is where every single state prisoner in New Jersey is sent, regardless of offense. There, they are categorized and ultimately shipped off to their "home" prison to spend the remainder of their time until the state considers them "rehabilitated."

From there, many are sent to halfway houses where they have much more freedom and temptation to break parole. Then, they get arrested and start the entire process all over again. That's why a few of my fellow prisoners at the detention center were able to at least try to prepare me for CRAF—they'd been there before. But CRAF just wasn't a place you could prepare for.

"The fuck does that say?"

I heard the guard's voice, but I was still staring at a brick wall during our group strip-search. Was he talking to me or one of the other five guys standing next to me?

We turned back around and one of the guards took a step closer to me.

"What's that tattoo say?"

"The one on my back?"

"Yeah."

"Robore et Vigiliantia."

"That Spanish or somethin'?"

"Latin."

"Latin? Who the fuck knows Latin?"

He looked more intently at my eyes while I stood in front of him. "What's it mean?"

"Strength through vigilance," I said, thinking of the tattoo for one of the first times since I'd gotten it four years earlier.

I was told it was my family motto; that centuries before my grandfather sailed to America as a young child my ancestors were herders and farmers in the Scottish highlands. As was common at the time, their wives and daughters were raped and what little they had was stolen. They did not want to fight, but they did. Sometimes they died. I was told their resolve grew stronger the more they fought back and, somewhere along the line, the phrase stuck.

"Oh, you're some sort of vigilante huh?" he said, pointing me out to the other guards with a smirk. "Guess we better keep an eye on this one."

I should've kept my damn mouth shut.

+++

The New Jersey Department of Corrections is the second

largest employer among state government agencies, with some 10,000 people "building rewarding careers," according to the departments website. Two weeks in, I was getting to know the kind of people that found this line of work "rewarding."

To be hired as a corrections officer, a candidate must be a high school graduate, at least eighteen years old, and speak English. They must also have a valid driver's license and must meet certain residency requirements. Candidates for these jobs are warned that they will be screened for such things as employment, domestic violence and driving histories. "Candidates will be given a through medical and psychological examination," the department states, "and must provide urine samples to determine drug use."

In March 2013, one of those successful candidates, a guard assigned to my new home in Trenton, was arrested on charges that he identified himself as a police officer in an attempt to coerce prostitutes into having sex with him—for free.

Investigators said Juan R. Stevens, a 50-year old senior corrections officer, supposedly telephoned women who advertised their services online under the name "Rich" or "Rick" to arrange for sexual encounters at hotels in Burlington County and Philadelphia. He would then meet the women for sexual acts and refuse to pay the price, instead insisting he was a police officer and displaying a badge that would make the women fear being arrested.

Officials also say that Stevens sometimes even carried handcuffs in his back pocket.

I guess the job did come with some "rewards," after all.

I spent my first few hours at CRAF sitting in a big metal cage with at least fifty other convicted felons. Lunch had already come and gone, so I missed my chance to have a carton of warm milk and a slice of bologna and cheese on white bread. I wasn't entirely upset about missing lunch, which was usually just enough painfully bland calories to keep the basal metabolism moving along for another day of meaningless existence.

As if the taste wasn't bad enough, the guys at County had filled my head with stories about inmates being poisoned and experimented on over the years by the government. I had no idea if any of it was true, but something about my experience with the government so far told me there might be some truth to all of the rumors. I watched guys pour out their juice—they'd only drink water from the tap.

"Don't drink that shit, man. They put saltpeter in it to make you sterile," my red-haired albino had told me early on.

A few days before I took the trip to Trenton, I asked Jenna to check into the rumors for me.

"So, millions of results pop up when you Google 'poison

prison food,'" Jenna said to me over the payphone.

"OK, like what?"

"Well, a *New York Times* article from 1861 says fifty prisoners in Brooklyn became violently ill from poisoned water."

"OK, well that was like a hundred years ago. Anything else? Some guys told me they put stuff in the water to make you sterile."

"Yeah, I saw that. Hold on, let me find it."

Seconds seem like hours when you're waiting to find out if there's a chance the water you're drinking might make you shoot blanks for the rest of your life.

"OK, got it. It looks like that's called saltpeter, a mix of potassium nitrate and sulfur, annnnd it's supposed to get rid of your sex drive. But it doesn't look like they actually do it? I don't know. It looks like an urban legend."

"Thanks, is there..."

"Wait," she cut me off. "There's a book called *Acres of Skin* about some doctor who did medical experiments on prisoners in Philadelphia."

She paused.

"It's old though. The experiments were done between 1951 and 1974..."

Jenna's voice cut off, and after another long pause she suggested, "Maybe just don't eat anything?"

It sounded crazy to me at the time, but Jenna sent me articles that had been published by *The New York Times*, *Baltimore Sun*, and *PBS*. These weren't tin-foil hat wearing conspiracy theorists blogging from their mother's basement —they were Pulitzer Prize-winning institutions.

Later, I saw that the Associated Press came out with an article detailing medical experimentation of prisoners in the United States. According to the article (which dated from the 1960's), patients in Brooklyn had been injected with cancer cells. One prisoner in Philadelphia had a layer of skin removed from his back and had "very painful chemicals" applied to the raw flesh. This wasn't happening overseas in some third-world country, but right here in the land of the free.

In all, the article reported more than 1,200 prisoners in Philadelphia "willingly" allowed experiments to be conducted on them for shampoos, foot powders, deodorant, mind-altering drugs, radioactive isotopes, and dioxin. In the case of dioxin, the US Army wanted to see if the popular herbicide could be used as an effective weapon and the Dow Chemical Company footed the bill for the experiments. Dioxin became the primary ingredient in Agent Orange, which the army used liberally to defoliate hundreds of thousands of acres of dense jungle in Vietnam.

Unfortunately, they also indiscriminately dumped the Agent Orange on thousands of American troops who sat unknowingly under the paths of US planes overhead spraying the forest. Many of these soldiers later died of various cancers or became fathers of children born with severe disabilities.

In Connecticut, the AP article continued, mentally ill prisoners were injected with hepatitis. In Maryland, a pandemic flu virus was sprayed up the noses of prisoners. These examples, more than forty experiments on an untold number of patients and prisoners, came from medical journals published forty to eighty years ago.

In more recent years—between 2006 and 2010—the Center for Investigative Journalism found that 148 female inmates in California were sterilized in violation of state law.

I was starting to think that I had just as much to fear from my captors as I did from the unpredictable and violent detainees around me.

Sometime during my second or third day there, I was sent up to medical with the other new transfers. We sat on a wooden bench across the hallway from a group of nurse's offices where other inmates were being given injections and having blood drawn. All the rumors, urban myths, and AP headlines weren't doing me any favors as I watched guys file in and out with the standard bumps growing where their tuberculosis test had been injected.

I asked a number of nurses if I was legally required to have the injections and was told by each that if I refused they would simply drug me and give me the vaccination under sedation. After signing a waiver, I was able to avoid having my blood drawn. I must have been one of the first people to request that, because the inmates and nurses all looked surprised when I requested the waiver. It took them thirty minutes to even find one so I could sign it.

I had grown hardened by the time I was shipped off to Trenton, and the inmates surrounding me didn't seem as threatening as they should have. The guards at CRAF were another story.

They would beat—and I am talking about face punched into the floor, knee in the back of the skull, don't see the guy ever again kind of beatings—inmates over the smallest of things, including something as innocuous as asking for a roll of toilet paper.

The toilet paper thing was a real problem. Inmates were not allowed to bring anything with them from their previous jail, including toiletries—and you couldn't get a new roll of toilet paper unless you handed in the cardboard tube from a used roll. That meant new guys couldn't get toilet paper because they didn't have a used roll to trade in. You'd expect they would've come up with a better system by now.

Shortly after I arrived I was taken aside by a guy on my wing and told the story of an inmate who'd had "an accident" after badgering one of the guards for toilet paper a couple weeks before I arrived.

Accidents happened.

If someone told my twenty-two year old self about all of this, I probably would have responded, "Who cares? If they wanted to be treated like humans they shouldn't have broken the law." Suddenly, I had a new perspective. With little exception, these were all still human beings—and I wasn't the only one who didn't deserve to be there.

At CRAF we spent more time in our cells than anywhere else. We shared our decrepit cells with rats, and spent our time reading smutty dime store novels and staring at the cracks in the ceiling, hoping it wouldn't collapse on us like other parts of the prison had already started to. We had a lot of time on our hands and nothing to do with it.

I couldn't receive letters or packages, and because everyone in CRAF is on their way to somewhere else, there were no real amenities. Worse, CRAF didn't allow any visitors, and the money on my account at the jail took weeks to transfer so, for most, there was no commissary. With no money on my account, there were no more comforting phone calls with Jenna or my parents. And that was the one thing I looked forward to every day.

The lack of communication with the outside meant I had no idea what my lawyers were up to or how far along the appeal had gotten, if they'd even filed it yet.

Most of the talk at CRAF focused on what permanent prison inmates would be assigned to. The guys on my block told me that, due to my age, I'd probably be assigned to either Bayside or Yardville. Neither had a good reputation.

Bayside was the prison George Wright escaped from back in 1970 after being convicted of murder. Two years later he helped hijack a Delta Air Lines flight and flew to Portugal where he's since evaded extradition to the United States. At CRAF, Bayside was better known for its indiscriminate violence.

"You don't wanna go to either of those places," one inmate told me, "They're both full of kids trying to make a name for themselves."

"Guys get stabbed there all the time," someone else added.

Lovely.

There was one place that didn't sound so bad called Jones Farm or, as the inmates affectionately referred to it, "The Farm." It supposedly supplied the milk to every single prison in the state and felons spent most of their days outside, surrounded by livestock and blue tent skies.

"You ain't goin' to no farm, bro," I was told, over and over.

"Nah, man, you're going to Bayside or Yardville. Best just lay low when you get there, but that probably won't do you any good, either."

Later, I was taken to a small room where a panel of strangers assigned inmates to their "home" prison. I sat on a plastic chair with a guard standing over me while they looked at a manila folder that I assumed was my file, or "jacket" as they called it in prison.

"Are you Brian Aitken?" one of the suits asked without looking up at me.

"Yes, sir."

They mumbled a little between themselves, still refusing to look at me, and all I could think was the worst. I knew all they saw were the words "guns," "hollow-points," and "high-capacity magazines." I really did not want to wind up lying in a pool of my own blood at Bayside with a sharpened spork sticking out of my kidney, just so some kid could be initiated into his gang.

But it wasn't up to me. It was up to these strangers who couldn't even bring themselves to look me in the eyes.

The guy in charge, who I assumed must have been the chairman of the committee, finally looked up.

"Mid-State Correctional Facility," he said over his tortoise shell glasses. "You can leave."

Mid-State? Nobody had said anything about a place called Mid-State. I walked out of the assignment room and asked the first guy I saw if he'd ever heard of it.

"Shit, man, that's where they send all the pedophiles."

"Shut the fuck up inmates!" the guard yelled at us.

Pedophiles. Perfect.

CHAPTER TWELVE

"Aitkens!" I heard the inmates yelling at me from my new bunk at the end of the tier, "Hurry up man! C.O.'s calling you!"

I threw my boots on and ran down to the end of the unit. My wing at Mid-State was one big dorm—no private cells—with nineteen bunk beds, housing thirty-eight prisoners. When I got to the end of the unit, the C.O. held out a copy of that morning's *Philadelphia Daily News* and pointed to the cover.

Beneath the masthead was a full page picture of my infant son hugging me at his first birthday party.

"Is this you?" he asked.

"Yes, that's me."

"That sucks man. Are you ok on this unit? You need anything?"

"No, I'm good."

"Ok, this is your buddy Jayson's so read it and get it back to me. You need anything you let us know."

He handed me the paper and I walked back to my bunk, eager to see what had been written. Jayson—my "buddy"—was Jayson Williams. At one time, he had been one of the highest-paid NBA players. Now he was serving time for manslaughter and lived on a wing across the hall from me. Williams was sentenced to two years less than I was, and his minimum mandatory sentence was only eighteen months—half the length of my mandatory minimum—even though he had taken a man's life with a shotgun.

I laid on my bunk and read the words the reporter had typed from his interview with me a week earlier. I had gotten a few requests to be interviewed while I was in prison—but Jason Nark was one of the only reporters who bothered to cover my story early on, so he was the only reporter I agreed to meet with in prison. He brought a staff photographer with him, and she seemed like a sweet girl, but I didn't want any more pictures of me in my khaki prison scrubs than already existed.

"It'll be powerful," they tried to convince me, "people will really sympathize with you if they see you in your prison clothes."

But I didn't want that to be an image my son would see one day. When you wear the uniform of a criminal people tend to assume you *are* a criminal, and I didn't want my son mistaking me for something I wasn't.

Nark's article ran under the headline:

NEW JERSEY MAN SERVING SEVEN YEARS FOR GUNS HE OWNED LEGALLY

Among the things Jason Nark called attention to in the piece was the fact that "the Burlington County Prosecutor's Office and the former Superior Court judge who tried the case ignored evidence that proved Brian had the guns legally."

The article also pointed out that Governor Christie had taken the unusual move of not renewing Judge James Morley's term: "A few weeks after Aitken's trial over the summer, Morley learned that Christie was not going to reappoint him, due in part to a 2009 case in which he dismissed animal-cruelty charges against a Moorestown cop accused of sticking his penis into the mouths of five calves."

Nark quoted Evan Nappen, who said he thought that the case "exemplifies poor decision-making by Morley... Brian didn't receive oral sex from calves; he only lawfully possessed firearms."

"Everybody wants to believe that there had to be something more to this case, but there's not," Nappen continued. "The judge made an error."

When Nark asked why I hadn't just taken the plea deal I answered, "When innocent people take a plea deal, they embolden prosecutors to pursue unjust convictions."

"This is the most normal, everyday, All-American regular kid," my dad was quoted, "and for this to happen to him is a disgrace. It's a disgrace of society."

The next day, an inmate came down to my bunk.

"Aitkens" he said, adding an s that isn't there, "C.O.'s callin' you. Warden wants to see you."

He turned around and walked away.

"Uh oh, man. What'd you do?" the overweight convict across from me asked as he sipped his jailhouse mocha—instant coffee blended with vanilla Ensure and peanut butter. "That's no good, man. You better hurry up."

I threw my clothes on and tucked my khaki shirt into my matching khaki pants and hustled down to the iron gate.

"Aitken?" the guard asked.

"Yessir"

"Come with me, warden wants to see you."

We walked down the hallway past the mess hall and the commissary to a small group of windowless offices with cinderblock walls. My escort introduced me to another officer.

"This him?" the new cop asked.

"Yep, that's Aitken," he said before walking away.

The new officer looked at me. "Have a seat, the warden's waiting."

For months I'd been nothing but a number. I'd been stripped of everything that made me human and wasn't used to people calling me by name. For the first time, I was treated like an actual person. Someone who had been a kid once. Who had dreams of greater things to come. Who had a family.

The warden appeared at the entrance to his office and stuck his hand out. I looked at it, not knowing what to do, and eventually shook it. There was a pretty strict no-contact rule in prison. They touched you. They patted you down. They strip-searched you. They pushed you up against the wall and kicked your feet apart. You did not touch them.

"Have a seat," he said, gesturing to the leather chair in front of his desk.

I looked down and saw a copy of the *Philadelphia Daily News* with my picture on the cover next to his morning coffee.

"Aitken. You're not supposed to be down here, so you're not, got it?"

"Yessir."

"Listen, me and some of the other guys, we think it's bullshit what happened to you. There's not a whole lot I can do but we can move you somewhere safer than where you're at. There's a wing that's pretty low-key. I can move you to it tonight if you want. You just have to fill out this request form."

He slid a form across the desk to me.

I looked down at it and wondered what those inmates on the other unit were like. I knew the guys on my unit, all thirty-seven of them. I knew who was dangerous. I knew who could be an ally. I had deals with some of them to help take care of me. Some had trade agreements with me to make sure I got enough stamps, pens, and envelopes. I was only allowed ten stamps a week and that wasn't nearly enough to keep up with the hundreds of letters I was receiving from people I had never even met.

The danger I knew seemed safer than a danger I didn't know.

"Thank you, but I'm ok where I'm at."

"Alright, let me know if you change your mind. Anyone gives you any trouble you just tell one of the C.O.'s and they'll tell me. Got it?"

"Yessir."

"Alright." He looked out his office door to a guard standing out there, "Take him back to his unit."

My new prison was surrounded by a twelve-foot-high fence topped with barbed wire laced with swirling rows of razor-sharp steel ribbon. On the other side of that chain-link fence was the Fort Dix Army base. Occasionally, we caught sight of a military cargo plane and heard the explosions of war games in the distance.

Mid-State housed prisoners who had already spent the majority of their time in a "real prison" and were preparing to be released. My fellow inmates included several Bloods, a thief who had stolen hundreds of exotic cars and sold them to South American chop shops, an old man convicted of financial fraud waiting to be sent to federal prison, and an uncomfortably large number of pedophiles and sexual offenders.

It was a place for people who needed to be protected from "General Population" at real prisons. Everyone there was close enough to being released that they put their almost instinctive violence on hold. I was told if a lawyer, judge, or cop was sent to prison he was sent to Mid-State. I wasn't sure how I wound up there but it felt like someone was looking out for me.

In prison there are no secrets. Everyone knows the crime

you're in for, but here there was a heightened awareness. Nobody wanted to accidentally become friends with a pedophile. They were marked men. In prisons around the world pedophiles have been beheaded, disemboweled, or just had their throats slit on the way to yard after they'd gotten too comfortable with their surroundings.

Because Mid-State had a much higher concentration of pedophiles than any of the other prisons in New Jersey, people hung their rap sheets on the lockers that stood next to their bunks. Even criminals have a sort of perverse moral code, and it all seems to revolve solely around pedophilia. In the world of prison, if you were in for murder, robbery, drugs, or possession of guns you had nothing to hide from. If you came across a locker without a rap sheet on it, you knew whoever slept there had done something horrible— and you knew enough not to associate with them.

I learned to exist within these contortions of morality, and I learned how to get through each day, but I never adjusted to prison life.

One inmate, an older white guy in his late forties named Dave, described the adjustment to life in prison as being "institutionalized." He had been in prison for years, and still had years left. He fought every day to keep himself from becoming "institutionalized," but in some ways that's what actually made him more so than everyone else. Some days he just freaked the fuck out over nothing. You could tell something was lost inside him and that, no matter how hard he fought it, he had already lost his former self.

"Don't you do it. Don't you start calling things what they call them in here. Don't eat the shit they make with the ramen and that fuckin' mackerel," he said in the beginning of one of his manic fits. I sat on my foot locker, silently, both of us wearing matching gray sweatsuits. He watched intensely as I made a jailhouse mocha. It tasted like shit, but it was the closest we got to Starbucks on the inside.

He stared at me, serious as cancer, "You drink that shit and you're gonna wind up like them. You don't wanna wind up like them. They're all fucking nuts in here."

He rattled these words off in a hushed whisper, every word faster than the last.

He was going insane.

Crazy or not, Dave watched my back. He made sure I had clothes and earplugs, which we weren't allowed to have. They were one of the things that really kept me sane. I'd wear them almost all day long just to tune out the sounds of guys yelling at the TV. The other inmates didn't like it. They thought it was rude, but I was beyond caring. I was just trying to survive.

If I needed anything, Dave would help me get it and he never asked for anything in return. He had connections. He got Cuban cigars, ear plugs, and just about anything else you could imagine. He was the guy you went to if you needed something. He was a trader. He didn't care about drama and didn't get involved in other peoples gossip or bullshit. He was one of the few guys I almost actually trusted in there. Almost.

We promised never to contact each other outside of prison under any circumstances.

"You don't deserve to be here. When you get out, don't send anybody a letter, don't accept any collect calls from any of these assholes. Put this bullshit behind you and move on with your life."

Some days I would go out to yard and lift weights or run around the dirt track. Most days, though, I stayed inside while almost everyone else went out. It was one of the few opportunities I had to be alone and have some privacy. I used the time to read the many books people sent me. I was averaging three books a week—catching up on years of neglected reading.

While I was rotting away on the inside, Jenna and my family had started a "Free Brian Aitken" Facebook page. In a matter of days it had attracted 16,000 'fans' who built a community around the singular goal of getting me out of prison. They talked with my family, shared stories about what they were doing to help, and mentioned any time they called or wrote a politician on my behalf. The phone calls and emails were starting to flood Governor Christie's office. Keep in mind this was 2010. That kind of activism wasn't really happening on Facebook the way it does now.

Out of desperation, I asked my lawyers to file the paperwork for executive clemency. Clemency is the power of the President or Governor to pardon or shorten the sentence of a person convicted of a crime. It's typically granted if there's a substantial doubt about the actual guilt of the incarcerated, if the sentence is excessive, on humanitarian grounds, or if the person is a political friend of the Governors. It's incredibly rare for any inmate to be granted clemency of any kind, though that doesn't stop tens of thousands of people from seeking it every year. Less than one-half of a percent of all requests are honored.

I specifically did not request a "pardon" from the governor, because a pardon carries with it the presumption of guilt. I did not want to beg forgiveness for a crime I did not commit.

My goal in requesting clemency was to be released and begin working on clearing my name and reputation—and to get back the right to see my son.

Several people submitted letters in support of the petition to the governor. But we could only include a handful.

> Dear Governor Christie,
>
> I'm writing to you about Brian Aitken who

was placed in the New Jersey prison system this past August.

I am currently a Nursing major at Ramapo College of New Jersey, specializing in Art Therapy and Psychiatrics. Simultaneously, I am a starting player for the Women's Volleyball Team, am an active member for the college's Women's Center, and am a volunteer for Strengthen Our Sisters, a shelter for victims of domestic violence.

Brian has been a good friend of mine since we met in the early summer of 2009 while on a trip to upstate New York. From the start, it was evident that Brian was a very compassionate person.

At the time of our meeting, I was going through a very rough patch in my life. I had just finished a civil court case with an ex-boyfriend who had sexually assaulted me two years previously while also dealing with the death of my grandfather, whom I was extremely close to. It was very difficult for my psychologically and emotionally. While being clinically depressed with an anxiety disorder and a failed suicide attempt two months prior, meeting Brian at this dark time of my life was a blessing. I felt extraordinarily comfortable opening up to him, something I did not do often.

While in New York, Brian offered to take me hiking in a beautiful section of the Catskill Mountains, known to the locals as "The

Gunks." While we were hiking he would explain the local flora, fauna, and surrounding areas with great knowledge which proved extremely therapeutic for me.

Not only did we go hiking, but he introduced me to a passion of his—mountain climbing. At first I was frightened because I am afraid of heights. Just the thought of being at the top of a mountain, hundreds of feet above the treetops, only supported by a bundle of ropes, was terrifying. Brian reassured me that I would be safe and surely enough I let him strap me in and belay me off. Once I started, I could not stop because it was so exhilarating. Brian talked me through the entire climb. At certain points when I felt weak, I could hear him say from below, "Just hold on, you've got this. Just hold on." When I did reach the top, he told me to look around and to see where I was. The view was completely breath-taking. Never have I had anyone help me feel so alive.

To this day, when things get tough, I can hear Brian telling me to hold on; to stop and look at where I am and how far I have come. He taught me to trust again and how there is so much more to live for. Brian talked me through panic attacks, kept me company during sleepless nights, and chased away my dark thoughts. He is my best friend, becoming more and more like a brother. Still, he remains humble and gives all the credit away. Though he reassures me that I made it with my own personal strength, I know that I

would not have made it to where I am today
without him.

I, however, was not the only one whose life
was touched. He took time out of every day
to care for his elderly neighbor who had
become very sick. He made sure there was
always food in the house, took him to
doctors' appointments, and periodically
checked on him throughout the day. If he,
for some reason, was not home, Brian made
certain that someone else was available to
care for him. Along with his compassionate
characteristics, he is a very successful student
and a CEO of a small business, Alister &
Paine, Inc. While attending Rutgers
University, he displayed a level of dedication
to this studies rarely seen of his peers of
undergraduates. During this time he also
made it a point to attend extra classes and
educational seminar at prestigious institutes
such as the University of Pennsylvania and
New York University. Even while
incarcerated, he is looking to earn his MBA
from the Manchester Business School. Brian
is obviously a very ambitious individual with
a strong work ethic, striving to accomplish
every goal he sets for himself with the
utmost persistence and dedication.

I now ask you this: why imprison someone
who displays so strongly the qualities that are,
and have always been, valued in our
American society? Brian is not in any way a
threat to society and, based solely on facts
and support by his personal background, is

no criminal.

Please think of Brian's family and friends who are now living life without him, and more so, think about his two-year-old son who has been left to grow up without his father.

Dwayne Carter was quoted in Rolling Stone magazine in February of 2009, stating: *"We're here to do. We're here to live. We're here to be... When it's over, man, it's over."* Allow Brian Aitken to do, to live, to be. He does not deserve to be locked up in prison surrounded by murderers and rapists. The crime he was convicted for is a non-violent and victimless one. Why keep him from his previous life? Why keep him from making a difference in others' lives, as he did for me? Society could use a man like him for his knowledge, hard work, dedication, and integrity.

I hope you take my words into consideration, as well as others who vouch for him, to pardon him from his incarceration.

Sincerely,

Katelyn M. Ward

As word of my innocence spread throughout the prison, some of the inmates began to treat me differently. To several guys on the tier I no longer "belonged" and they were secretly angered that I was there—not just because I was innocent, but because they felt judged every time they saw me. I suppose, when you're guilty it's easier to be surrounded by other people who are guilty. The suffering is somehow worse with the knowledge that an innocent man is watching your pathetic life play out every second of every day.

What they didn't understand was that I was punching the timecard of the same pathetic existence they were. It wasn't living. No one was alive in there. We just existed. And we hardly existed at all.

Mail-call had turned into a daily Christmas morning with dozens of letters arriving from around the world. At first, everyone on the tier was excited to see what state or country someone had written me from. Florida. Delaware. Texas. New Hampshire. California. Colorado. England. Australia. Afghanistan. Letters poured in from all corners of the map. After a while, the excitement of my fellow inmates turned to pain as they remembered their girlfriends who hadn't visited them in months and their children who hadn't written them in years.

I became more guarded when mail-call came around. I didn't want these guys to suffer any more just because they shared a tier with me—incarceration was punishment enough without the constant reminder that many of them had been abandoned and long forgotten. Not only that, but I'd been warned that certain inmates would memorize return addresses and personal details from letters sent by loved ones so they could extort money from you. "Pay up or your mother gets it," kind of stuff. I kept my mail locked away from my felonious neighbors.

Perhaps the single most important and transforming media event came from talk radio host Dennis Malloy of NJ101.5, who dedicated a two-hour show to my case on my twenty-seventh birthday.

I borrowed some headphones and listened to the broadcast lying down in my bunk. Other inmates tuned in from all over the prison. The guys on my unit congratulated me and asked me if I thought Christie would let me out. They asked if I was really innocent.

"That fucking judge man, he had it out for you," one told me.

I heard Dennis Malloy's voice.

"I seriously need your help," he told his listeners. "I want you to get anybody you know to listen to this show. Tweet them, text them, email them. I'm going to tell a story about someone who's in jail who shouldn't be. And it could happen to any one of us.

I'm gonna introduce to you now a guy named Larry Aitken. Larry is a resident of Mount Laurel, New Jersey. I spoke to him for the first time last night on the phone after hearing his story about his twenty-six year old son who is celebrating his birthday in jail today. He was sentenced to seven years in jail. The kid's never committed a crime in his life. Clean record. Upstanding citizen. A good guy. And he's in jail. Could be you. Could be me. Could be a relative of someone we know."

My dad explained what had happened, "The short version of a long story is that my son graduated Rutgers and wanted to live in Colorado. So, he moved with his college sweetheart and did what everyone strives to do; got a job, bought a house, had a son. Was living the normal all-American everyday life."

Malloy listened, interjecting an occasional question and offering his stunned disbelief.

"Please don't tune out," Dennis pleaded, "Please listen to this story. Please. Please. Please. Please. I've never asked you to do this before. Never. I want you to listen to this story and I want you to do what you can to help. Write to the governor's office. Flood their email and their phone lines. I know there have been other miscarriages of justice throughout the history of the State, but this is heinous. This is important. This is wrong."

I heard my mothers frail voice through the foam padding of the dated AM/FM Walkman. I heard the regret in the crackle in every word she spoke. I felt my mother's pain as I heard her fight to keep from crying on live radio.

"I just wanted to say," she said, taking a deep breath to stay the frustration, anger, and tears, "that this has been really hard. It's been two months since he's been in jail. Today's his twenty-seventh birthday. I've sent him a card every day so that he gets one on his birthday..."

She tried to explain why she had called the cops that night in Mount Laurel.

"I'm sure, Sue, you place a lot of guilt on yourself for this," Malloy said.

"Of course. I try not to think about that."

I could hear her crying now.

"I just can't believe that my son took the proper precautions and the police officers offered to give me the guns that night and have me store them in my house. And if the police officers don't know the law, you expect my son to know the law? And then they put him in handcuffs and took him away!"

Hearing my mother cry for me, in front of millions of listeners, was worse than anything that had happened so far.

But it got worse for her.

People blamed her for everything that happened.

An article published after Dennis' show aired led with the fact that my mom had called the cops on me.

"Sue Aitken called the police because she was worried about her son, Brian. She now lives with the guilt of knowing that her phone call is the reason Brian spent his 27th birthday in a New Jersey prison last month. If the state gets its way, he will be there for the next seven years."

The backlash from Monday morning quarterbacks was brutal.

"Fuck the judge, fuck the jury, fuck the cops, and fuck his mother... Whatabitch," wrote one online respondent.

"I did it because I love you, not because I'm thinking rationally. Which actually translates to I'm an emotional retard who dialed 911 and then hung up. This guy deserves a metal for putting up with his bitch ex, and still talking to his retard mother," wrote another.

This wasn't her fault.

The fault was my own.

I was the one who didn't see my ex-wife for who she really was and, instead, was blinded by who I thought she had the potential to be. Had I been wiser, I never would have found myself in the situation that unraveled on that cold January day five years ago. But then, I wouldn't have a beautiful son out there somewhere. He's one of the greatest gifts I've ever been given. And I know one day, after lots of explaining, emotion, and healing, he and I could have the relationship we both deserve.

Not long after my birthday a beat-up postcard with a desert mountainscape on the front made it to me. The photograph was titled "Mulakhail of Panjshir Province" and the postcard had a return address from Kandahar Airfield in Afghanistan. On the back, scribbled in black ink, an American military officer wrote:

> Mr. Aitken,
>
> I heard of your plight via Reddit and was appalled at your treatment, arrest and conviction on such bogus charges. I wish that I could do more than write a postcard to you and the Governor.
>
> You know your story must really suck when you're getting a sympathy card from a war zone!
>
> So while I'm over here trying to bring a modicum of security and freedom to this third world country, your freedom has been stripped away by some of my fellow citizens at home.
>
> Keep your spirits up my friend, this can only get better! Happy Birthday!
>
> Just know that you have a lot of people behind you in this fight and your case will not be forgotten or allowed to be swept under the rug.

Keep your head high and watch your back.

Sincerely,

Captain Bryan Zeski

Each and every letter meant a lot to me, but knowing he had taken time from his war-torn day to write had validated my choice to stand and fight.

October passed quickly into November and the number of stories about my fight for freedom increased in media outlets across the country. *The Philadelphia Daily News*, *The Trentonian*, the Newark *Star-Ledger*, Fox News, CBS, MSNBC, and dozens of blogs and forums were spreading the word.

Even Wayne LaPierre, president of the National Rifle Association, wrote an impassioned piece entitled 'Free Brian Aitken':

> The story of Brian Aitken, the 27-year-old currently serving a seven-year prison sentence in New Jersey for the "crime" of having his legally owned firearms locked up and unloaded in the trunk of his car, has garnered a lot of mainstream media attention over the past few days, and rightfully so. His story is incredible, from the judge who refused to let Brian's jury hear about exemptions in New Jersey's draconian gun laws that allowed him to legally transport his firearms while moving, to the fact that Aitken checked with the New Jersey State Police before moving specifically to ensure that he

would be in compliance with state law, to the pathetic argument offered by Ceasefire NJ's Bryan Miller that Aitken must be lacking in "common sense."

Is it common sense to put a man behind bars for most of a decade, simply because a judge decided he didn't meet the definition of "moving"? Is it common sense that every New Jersey gun owner faces the same sentence if they dare commit the heinous crime of stopping to get gas or a cup of coffee on their way to and from the range?

Governor Chris Christie can't do anything by himself to change New Jersey's unjust gun laws, but he can do something to ensure justice for Brian Aitken. A petition for clemency has been presented to the governor, and it's my fervent hope that he will act on it. The NRA's Civil Rights Defense Fund is helping to pay for Brian Aitken's appeal, and we will continue to support legal efforts to free Aitken from his sentence, but the governor can act much more quickly than the courts. Every day that Mr. Aitken wakes up in a prison cell instead of his own home is another day that justice is delayed and denied.

By late November, a state-wide second amendment organization announced plans for a rally in Toms River to "raise awareness of the plight of Brian Aitken, and to petition Governor Christie to grant Brian clemency and release him before Christmas."

The momentum was snowballing and I thought the rally would help increase awareness about my incarceration and the insidious legal charades that brought me there.

From my limited view in the confines of Mid-State, it looked like the rally began to take on a different shape. I was receiving worried messages from friends that the event was becoming less about "freeing Brian Aitken" and more about "keeping your damn hands off my guns." My parents and family members—who had previously been at the top of the list of speakers—were bumped in favor of gun rights advocates from across the country. Strategically speaking, if the rally happened before Governor Christie acted on my case, his opponents could easily have spun the story against him—headlines would read "Christie caves to gun rights advocates," and there was no way this governor was going to "cave" to anyone. He was too good of a politician to let that happen.

To the disappointment of many well-meaning people, I pulled my support from the rally. Christie had been contemplating a number of requests to grant me clemency, not just from my lawyers and the growing number of supporters called into action by Dennis Malloy and others, but also from state legislators.

As Thanksgiving drew near, New Jersey assemblyman Michael Patrick Carroll wrote a public plea to the governor asking him to "immediately pardon, or commute the sentence of, Brian Aitken, getting him out of jail so that he can spend the holidays with his family." The assemblyman continued, "He threatened no one, his conduct presented no matter of public concern. And, yet, while numerous real criminals receive sentences amounting to little more than slaps on the wrist for felonies which threaten public safety, Brian received a mandatory sentence of seven years, much of it without parole, representing a gross miscarriage of justice... That this case reached this point is astonishing. And outrageous."

A phone call came with news that the governor had mentioned me during a press conference.

From the back of the room, out of the sight of the cameras, a reporter stood up and asked one simple and poignant question.

"Have you received a request to intercede before the appellate hearing and do you think it's right that you should?"

"Yes," the governor replied from behind the State seal of New Jersey, "representatives on behalf of Mr. Aitken have filed a formal request for pardon. My counsel's office has put together documents that I've begun to review and I would suspect that I'll be in a position to make a decision on whether or not I'll intervene prior to Christmas."

Those forty-nine unimpassioned and carefully chosen words

changed everything.

CHAPTER THIRTEEN

Christie's popularity was growing across the country. Pundits on every major network were wondering if he was gearing up for a presidential bid in 2012, and I felt like the future of a kid from a small town in South Jersey wasn't at the top of his list.

I knew he wasn't going to do anything unless I was thoroughly vetted and that he was only going to intervene if it was in his best interest. He could easily tell the media my case was before the Appellate Division and, out of respect for the legal process, he was not going to get involved. That would be the safe thing to do. The political thing to do.

"You think Christie's really gonna let you out?" my chubby bunkmate asked after returning from kitchen detail.

"I don't know."

"I dunno either, man. I dunno."

Chris seemed decent enough for the inside, and when you're inside that's all that matters. On the outside, who knew? I had no idea who he really was.

"That's a big risk for a governor. You know that, right? He's got a lot to lose."

Chris bent over and opened up his footlocker, pulling out a plastic bag of instant coffee.

"You want some?"

"No, I'm good."

I looked back down at a stack of letters I'd gotten that day. There were dozens. My daily mail call consisted of the weekday edition of the *Wall Street Journal* and a stack of letters. My dad had gotten me a subscription to the *Journal* so I could still feel connected to my past life. Jenna's dad, a proud "independent" and British expat—who leaned uncomfortably close to socialist ideals—got me a subscription to the Sunday edition of the *New York Times*.

At first, inmates lined up for a chance to see the periodicals after me. They organized a system that determined who would get it first, second, third and so on. I made sure Dave got it first, since he hooked me up with the earplugs that kept me sane. If Chris was around, he got the paper next. After that I didn't care.

When the guys realized there weren't really any pictures in the *Wall Street Journal* they stopped lining up. It never dawned on me until then that a lot of them could barely read, and that they had just been looking at the pictures all along. In that respect, the *Journal* didn't have a lot to offer.

Out of nowhere my mail began to double and triple, undoubtedly a result of the media firestorm lit by Governor Christie's press conference.

One of the envelopes contained an early Christmas card from Arizona with a drawing of an ethereal angel holding a harp on the front.

> Hi Brian,
>
> You have no idea how many people there are out here fighting for your freedom. I'll be calling Governor Christie's office every week until you are free. Oh, and we've got friends who'll help us, too!
>
> Your friends in Arizona,
>
> Randy & Barbara

I'd gotten dozens of cards like Randy and Barbara's by that time. I had never felt so alone, yet so completely surrounded by love and friends before in my entire life. I put the card down on my footlocker and opened a letter from Houston.

Brian,

My thoughts & prayers go out to you and
your family. The injustice bestowed on you is
incomprehensible. What further disturbs me
is this appears to stem from a visitation
denial.

Parental interference is another injustice the
authorities turn their heads at. How does this
help your child? 7 years? Insanity!

May you keep your head high & know <u>you
are not the criminal</u>! Nothing in the
constitution says you have to have permission
to carry a firearm.

May you seek some happiness during this
holiday. You are a true hero for moving
closer to your son in New Jersey. I will be
calling Christie's office as well. Take care, stay
strong, Don't waiver!

Michael

P.S. A piece of Texas is behind you!

A blade of grass was taped to the letter. I was getting a lot of
letters from people in Texas. Most of them encouraged me
to move there after I got out and, I have to say, that didn't
sound like such a bad idea to me at all.

Despite what that letter from Texas had said, I didn't feel like
a hero. I felt like a failure. I failed at marriage. I failed at
fatherhood. By the time Brennan got around to me, I was

just a guy with nothing left to lose.

I put that letter down with the other and heard Chris's voice again.

"Say Christie lets you out," he hypothesized while pulling lunchmeat out of his work boot. "Say he lets you out and you do something. You fuck up. Anything, you kill a guy by accident. Get a DUI or something."

He pulled a bag of bread out of his pants.

"That's political suicide for a guy like Christie. He's got too much to risk, man."

Chris made eye contact with me for the first time since he got back from the kitchen. I just stared back at him, emotionless.

"I'm sorry, man," he said, pouring the instant coffee into the plastic cup with his name written on the side, "I just don't want you getting your hopes up. That's dangerous."

"Thanks, Chris." I said. "I gotta write back to some of these people. Do you have any more stamps I can borrow?"

"Sure, sure. Whatchu got?"

I looked in my footlocker. I had three packs of loose tobacco and a few packets of mackerel.

"What do you want?"

"Give me two packs of mackerel and I'll give you fifteen stamps."

"Deal," I said, handing over the mackerel that I had I bought just for situations like this.

Stamps were hard to get. Inmates were only allowed a limited supply of stamps—ten a week—so I bought tobacco and mackerel even though I didn't smoke or eat fish. Then I'd trade with guys on the tier for pens, envelopes, legal pads, and stamps. Inbound mail had its stamps defaced with permanent marker so inmates couldn't reuse them. Stamps were our own fiat currency.

Every time a guard yelled out my name for mail call or weekend visit, my hopes rose a little bit higher, and I wondered if this was it—if this was the call that would get me out of prison. Weeks passed and my name was yelled dozens of times. The call from the governor never came.

I stopped hearing my name.

On the outside things were heating up despite the December chill. Judge Napolitano, whose FreedomWatch had really given my case its first breath of outside coverage, invited my parents on the show to appear as guests. It had become a popular weekly program on FOX Business and was attracting a far larger audience than when I had appeared on the internet-only version sixteen months earlier.

I had no say in what we watched on the tier so I didn't get to see my parents appearance on FOX. The one time I tried changing the channel, from BET to the History Channel, I almost got my ass kicked.

Fortunately, my sister had recorded the show on her DVR and played it back to me over the prison payphone. I could hear the Judge pleading for America to help.

> "The story of Brian Aitken is heartbreaking. Brian is a decent young man, and a law abiding citizen. He was arrested, charged, and locked up simply because he had guns which the state said he could lawfully possess. Keep e-mailing, keep calling, and keep praying that Governor Christie will do the right thing."

My parents and Jenna were planning a "Call to Action Day," on December 15, to have as many people as possible call their elected officials—including Chris Christie—and ask them to let me out of prison. They put out "the call" on Facebook and as many other social media sites as possible.

In the call to action, my family quoted Clark Neily, a senior attorney at the Institute for Justice—a public interest law firm like the ACLU, but more philosophically consistent— who told the Daily Caller, "This is the time to put up or shut up. Governor Christie has to decide if he's going to walk the walk on this one."

They asked everyone to be as polite as possible and to wish

the governor a Merry Christmas before begging him to do what only he had the power to do: release me from prison.

Thousands of people took to the phones to ask Governor Christie to commute my sentence and shared their experiences on the "Free Brian Aitken" Facebook page. Liberals. Conservatives. Anarchists. Libertarians. No matter where people sat on the gun-control issue, they seemed to know an injustice needed to be corrected.

> "Already called. I've never called a governors office for anything but this guy needs to be home for Christmas to see his child."—Mike Taffe

> "I placed my call and the aide was very kind and gracious. I told her that Alabama wants to see Brian home and free! I also told her we have been praying for Gov. Christie and wish all of the happy holidays."—Brandy Geier Musick

> "I called as well. The woman I spoke with was pleasant and seemed to appreciate the call."—Maria Martinez

So many people called that the phone lines to the governor's office crashed.

+++

"Aitken!" I heard the familiar shout from one of the guards at the end of the tier. I put my khakis on quickly, while most of the rest of my wardrobe dried over the end of my bunk. I did most of my laundry in the shower with a bar of soap, with the exception of my "nice uniform"—the clothes I wore when my family came to visit—which were cleaned by laundry services. Things had a way of disappearing when you sent them down to laundry. Nice clothes were swapped with tattered ones. To keep the guys honest, we would slip a pack of mackerel in with the laundry to make sure all of our washables made it back in one piece.

"You got more packages. You starting a library down there?" the C.O. asked as he unlocked the gate. He handed me a hall pass and I clipped it to my photo ID. "You know where it is. Down the hall, window on your left."

There were two packages waiting for me at the mailroom, both from Amazon. People couldn't personally send me books, but dozens of people had been ordering books online and sending them direct from the distributor. That day's package included a copy of Hunter S. Thompson's *Fear & Loathing on the Campaign Trail '72* and Robert Pirsig's *Zen and the Art of Motorcycle Maintenance*.

"Someone tried sending you chocolate," the mailroom guard said to me as I signed the paperwork confirming receipt of the delivery. "It's just a bag of holiday M&M's, but I can't give it to you."

Some chocolate would have been awesome right then. I'd been surviving off a peanut butter and jelly sandwich a day and those jailhouse mochas.

"Think anyone would really notice?" I asked.

"Sorry, Aitken. I want to, but it's my ass if you get caught."

"Alright," I gave him a look to see if he might leave the chocolate and turn a blind eye. He didn't. "Thanks anyway."

I walked back to my tier, turned in my badge, and hiked towards my bunk at the end of the wing.

Death stopped me.

"Hey yo! Whatchu got? Anything good?" Death asked.

"Just a couple of books," I replied.

"Books? Fuck man, chu know I can't read," Death said, taking the paper bag from me and looking inside. He handed back the bag and smiled.

"I jus kiddin' wichu, man. I kiddin'. I not gonna take yo stuff. You neecha hair done?"

Death was the tier's barber. For one pack of oily mackerel he'd cut your hair. He had a spider web tattooed on his elbow and a teardrop inked under his left eye. I didn't quite trust him with the razor and scissors.

"Not today, maybe before the weekend. Before my parents visit."

"Aight," Death said, never taking his eyes off mine. "Chu never look away, man," he said, tilting his head, examining me intensely.

"No, I guess I don't."

Death snapped out of it, remembering not to be hostile to paying customers, "Aight, I gonna cutchu Friday."

I hoped he meant I was getting a haircut, but he was genuinely insane and I don't think either one of us really knew what he meant.

Back at my bunk, I opened up my locker and put the new books inside. I jumped up to the top bunk, laid down, and pulled a book from under the pillow. *Where Men Win Glory* by Jon Krakauer, an account of the death in Afghanistan of former NFL star and Army Ranger Pat Tillman at the hands of his own colleagues.

It was the forty-first book I'd read in the past sixteen weeks.

I would try and read until lights-out and then I would pray. I didn't want to be a hypocrite, since I was sure I'd sinned too much to be allowed to pray for myself to a God I wasn't sure I really believed in—so instead I prayed for my family and for Jenna. Every night I told God to do what he wanted with me but to look after my mom, my son, and Jenna. I could take care of myself. I always had. But, I asked to cash in any favors I could if someone upstairs could keep an eye on them.

I had a hard time getting a good nights sleep in prison. The lights were never really turned off and someone was always awake doing something. It's difficult to get any REM sleep when the only thing separating you from thirty-seven convicts is a thin white sheet and a prison blanket.

I found myself thinking about Logan more and more. I wondered who was taking care of him and if he had a positive male role model or just men who came in and out of his life with the changing of the seasons. It wasn't just me who couldn't see him. My son's mother refused to let anyone in my family see him. Logan had a cousin who had just been born who he hadn't met yet. I wondered if they ever would.

"Brian, they're working on it," my father told me over the payphone, "Some of the governor's people met with your lawyers. Here, talk to your mother."

"Brian?"

I heard my mother's voice. Guarded and fragile.

"Hi, mom. How're you holding up?"

"I'm good, I'm good, you know..."

The strain in her voice was unbearable.

"OK, I love you. Here's dad."

"Hey, Brian."

"You were saying someone met with Richard and Evan?"

"Well, I don't know if it was a meeting or phone calls or what, but the governor's lawyers reached out to your lawyers. I think it's a good sign. I don't think Christie would've said anything at all if he didn't intend on doing something."

I looked at the paint peeling off the cinder block wall in front of me.

"Yeah, I guess you could be right. I'm worried there's a way for him to play it safe. To do something without actually doing anything."

"I've thought of that, too. There's a chance he could say he's looked into your case, and he feels for you, but that he won't intervene and will let the courts decide. He was a prosecutor, after all. He could show sympathy and not actually let you out of prison."

"Do you think he's that kind of guy? I asked.

"No," he said, "I don't."

The days were bleeding into each other and the air was growing colder. In the morning, frost would line the walls and by midday water dripped from the ceiling. Nothing really changed in prison during winter. It just got colder and darker in a place where I didn't think it was possible to get any colder or darker.

I decided to try and get some rest.

The stress of waiting was wearing me thin. Literally. My jailhouse diet of one peanut butter and jelly sandwich per day had left me twenty pounds lighter. I didn't feel any different, but my family was growing concerned about how skinny I looked.

I laid down on my bunk and pulled the torn sheets over my eyes to try and block out the glare from the fluorescent lights overhead. I started to fall asleep when I felt my bunk shaking violently.

"Yo!"

It was Rocco, the skin-head who'd been in a bike gang decades ago and still talked about his "old lady" and the Harley he hadn't even seen in years, let alone ridden.

"They're calling your name. Get dressed, man."

"What're you talking about, Rock?"

I looked at his black-and-gray beard, braided with a rubber band down to his chest. He was wearing a wife beater, gray sweatshorts, white gym socks, and orange rubber sandals with broken eyeglasses held together with white medical tape.

"I don't know what you did, but they seem pissed. The C.O.'s been calling your name for like five minutes."

It didn't take me long to look presentable. If you had to see a C.O., you always had to be in full uniform: khaki shirt over a white t-shirt, tucked into khaki pants with an elastic waistband, and white sneakers. I was dressed and at the gate in under two minutes.

"Aitken, come with me" the guard said, unlocking the steel gate.

"Where are we going?"

"They want you up at clinic. Did someone threaten you?"

The question caught me off guard. I tried to think of anyone who might want to hurt me. In prison, you just never knew. Tensions were always high beneath the surface. People snapped.

"No, not that I know of," I said while the faces of every inmate I knew flashed by, wondering who wanted to kill me. And why. "Not to my face, anyway."

"Well, you've got the whole prison up in a shitstorm. They're putting you in solitary. They only do that when there's a serious threat against an inmate's life."

"Here you go," the guard introduced me to the clinic sentinel, "This is Aitken."

The pair chaperoned me past the exam room where, weeks before, I reluctantly had my first dental exam in years, to a small cell with a solid steel door and a microscopic window.

There was no blanket, no pillow, no cellmate—just stone walls and the weighing curiosity of who might want to hurt me.

"Does someone really want to kill me?" I asked the clinics officer.

"Don't know. I don't know what's going on. They told us to get you off the tier, so you're off the tier."

"Ok," I looked around at the raw, unpainted, stonewalls.

"Do you think I could get a book? I was in the middle of reading a book, I'd like to finish it."

"No."

"Please, I've got nothing to read in here."

"You want a handbook? You can read the inmate's handbook if you want, I've got a copy of that."

"No, I just..."

The other guard, the one who walked me down off the tier, interrupted.

"Where is it? I'll get it."

"It's under my mattress."

"Ok, what's it called?"

"Civil Disobedience."

He stared at me for a few seconds longer, "Ok, I'll look for it."

He returned five minutes later, book in hand.

I sat back in my new cell, alone with Thoreau, and opened to where I'd left off that morning. The words stared back at me, relentless:

> "I was not designed to be forced. I will breathe after my own fashion. Let us see who is the strongest."

I wondered if this was it. If maybe the guards had made a mistake and if the governor was letting me out of prison. I was battle-weary and cold. There were no payphones in solitary, so I couldn't call Jenna as I usually did every night. Maybe the guards were wrong about the threat, I thought. I fell asleep, shivering but hopeful.

When I awoke the next morning I stared at the ceiling for what could have been hours. I thought it was still early but, without being able to see outside, I couldn't really tell.

I had gotten used to a routine that helped me keep track of the hours. On a typical day, my prison job was to clean the bathroom as soon as it was "lights on." I couldn't imagine a worse job than cleaning up the digestive aftermath of thirty-eight convicts. Shortly after I was done pulling the hair out of the drains and soaking the shower stalls in bleach, the TV would turn on and the inmates would line up in alphabetical waves for breakfast.

I had started paying people in tobacco to do my job for me, but my outsourcing wasn't sitting well with some of the guys on the tier, and trouble on the tier meant trouble with the guards. As it turned out, my addict subcontractors made horrible employees and many of the other inmates had begun to complain about how dirty the bathroom was. Certain "surprise" dinners made the bathroom reek like the port-a-potties at Burning Man after a week of idealists shitting out the consequences of too much molly and LSD.

With the complaints increasing, I was forced to fire my subcontractors and clean the semen-crusted showers myself.

In solitary, there was no TV and no trip to the mess hall for breakfast. The routine was gone and, consequently, so was any semblance of time. It could have been five in the morning or nearing noon.

I found myself staring at the wall, trying to make sense of the past two years. I couldn't figure out why my son had to grow up without his father or how the public benefited from my incarceration.

My concentration was broken by the heavy grinding of the guard opening the door to my cell. The light from the outside was blinding.

"Aitken," she said without the slightest inflection of emotion, "the governor called. You're leaving today."

CHAPTER FOURTEEN

"Who's Brian?" asked an unfamiliar female voice.

I looked up from my nap on the hospital couch, which seemed intentionally designed to keep people from getting too comfortable, to see the faces of Jenna's entire family staring at me. "I am. I'm Brian," I said, standing up and looking directly at the aide behind the familiar group.

"She's asking for you."

"Am I allowed back?"

"Yes, just follow me."

Jenna's mom, who'd been watching silently, asked in a frail but assertive voice, "Can I come, too?"

We walked back to the recovery room. Jenna was lying there, tucked beneath the hospital blankets, wearing the same surgical hairnet look she Snapchatted to all our friends just four hours earlier. Only now, she wasn't smiling.

The air in the hospital was stale and the linoleum tile depressing. Jenna was not completely conscious, and seeing her lying there beneath a tangle of oxygen support and intravenous fluids struck a weakness I hadn't felt since my son was born.

I dropped my guard long enough to let tears well up in my eyes. Those tears were different from my last ones, though. They weren't tears of joy at a beautiful life to come, but were indicative of an uncertainty of what's to come in the months and years ahead.

The surgeon had told me earlier that the mastectomy was successful but, as they had feared, the cancer had spread to her lymph nodes. Jenna asked if they had had to do an axillary dissection and I answered, "Yes." The look in her eyes said she understood but the drugs helped her forget and I will have to answer the same question a few hours later.

I leaned in to kiss Jenna's forehead and she opened her eyes and smiled at me. "I asked for you," she said in a raspy voice, searching for my hand with her pinky, fighting through the remnants of her recent anesthetization. "The first thing I said when I woke up was 'Where's Brian?'"

Jenna had always taken care of me. Just a few weeks earlier, as the test results began to sink in, I realized that the honeymoon was over and it was my turn to take care of her.

Looking down at my young bride, wrapped in hospital blankets, I thought about the last five years.

My mind flashed back to a week we spent in Florida together after my release from prison. Jenna had spent most of what should have been a fun and exhilarating week together taking care of me as I lay in bed unable to move. Unable to do anything. I had been living and working in San Francisco and she stayed behind in New York. We took turns flying to one another every other week. On this particular weekend in early 2012 we met in Miami for a weeklong workshop I was attending for my Global MBA program, which I was working on through the United Kingdom's Manchester Business School.

The day before boarding the plane at SFO I received a manila envelope with Evan Nappen's familiar return address label. Inside was the verdict from the New Jersey Appellate Division. I read it on the plane.

Two of the three convictions had been overturned—including the most damning: Illegal Possession of Firearms. I was still a convicted felon, and entitled to all the inglorious and demeaning things that went along with the title: failed background checks, extra scrutiny on apartment applications, and sideways glances from new clients unsure if they should bring up my infamy.

The two-judge panel's decision read, in part:

> Defendant Brian D. Aitken appeals his conviction for second-degree unlawful possession of a weapon, in violation of N.J.S.A. 2C:39-5(b) (count one), fourth-degree possession of a large capacity ammunition magazine, in violation of N.J.S.A. 2C:39-3(j) (count two), and fourth-degree possession of prohibited ammunition (hollow nose bullets), in violation of N.J.S.A. 2C:39-3(f)(1) (count three). We reverse the convictions on counts one and two, but affirm the conviction on count three.

I was overwhelmed and underwhelmed all at once. What do you do when it's over? Was it over? Could I take the last point to the Supreme Court of New Jersey? Could I take it to the U.S. Supreme Court? I was left with too many unanswered questions. It seemed like an incomplete victory, if it was a victory at all.

The Appellate Division determined I had been denied due process because the judge refused to instruct the jury on the exemptions for the most serious charge:

> We hold that the judge should have instructed the jury on the exemptions and that his failure to do so was "capable of producing an unjust result." Consequently, we

reverse the conviction on count one.

But, their logic didn't extend to the exemptions that governed the possession and transportation of hollow-point ammunition. When I read the jury requests, it was obvious the jury was asking for all of the exceptions to all of the charges... and not just the one.

> "Please define the exceptions to the law for all three charges. That is it was announced that 'moving is an exception.' We need to be clear of all exceptions, if any, for each charge."

It didn't make sense that the Appellate judges would throw out one charge based on the judge's refusal to provide the exceptions and wholly ignore the others.

Normally, I don't have trouble flying. I climb mountains, jump out of perfectly good planes, and snowboard the deep powder of the backcountry. But the plane on the way to Miami was getting smaller, the air was getting thicker and harder to breathe. I looked around to see if anyone noticed my anxiety, then wondered if anyone had ever gotten news like this on a commercial airplane before. I kept flipping through the pages Nappen had sent, searching for why the judges had refused to overturn the ammunition conviction. A part of me wondered if they just wanted a conviction to stand—any conviction—to keep me from filing a civil lawsuit and to justify the actions of everyone involved.

What I found was unbelievable. Near the very end of their decision the judges wrote, "There simply is no exception for moving between residences in the statute."

The exemptions for possessing firearms and hollow-point ammunition in New Jersey are practically identical. Practically, but not entirely. And that was the problem. That was why I was still a convicted felon. There is no specific exemption in New Jersey statutes that allows law-abiding gun owners to take their legally purchased hollow-point ammunition from their prior place of residence to their new residence. It felt like an oversight; like sloppy legislation and not at all consistent with the spirit of the law.

They decided that while it is legal for someone to purchase hollow-points in New Jersey, and legal for that person to take the ammunition from the store where they bought it to their house, it's not legal for that same person to take the ammunition to their new house when they move.

But the exemption also specifically states:

> "Nothing in subsection [(f)](1) shall be
> construed to prevent a person from keeping
> such ammunition at his dwelling."

Wasn't the Appellate Division's decision preventing me from keeping that ammunition at my new dwelling by making it illegal for me to move it there?

Even Judge Morley couldn't tell the two exemptions apart.

During the trial, the judge argued the hollow-point exemptions were identical to the firearm exemptions, and so they didn't need to be specifically included in the charge to the jury:

> "It's the same exemption, right? It's legal to bring it from one legal place to another legal place as long as it's packaged the right way, correct?"

If a sitting judge can't even tell the statues apart, how on earth do they expect a common citizen to?

In one fell swoop they set a legal precedent turning thousands of gun owners in New Jersey into potential felons when they move to a new home with their legally purchased ammunition.

What exactly are New Jersey residents supposed to do with the ammunition, I wondered. It seemed irresponsible to just leave it behind at the former residence; who knows whose hands it might end up in. It appeared the Appellate Division wanted people to simply abandon hollow-point ammunition all over the State of New Jersey instead of moving it discretely, locked in the trunk of a car, to their new home.

CBS News was one of the many media outlets that announced the decision, noting that my case had become a "cause celebre among gun-rights advocates."

The county prosecutor's office quickly issued a statement

that it would not try to reconvict me:

> "Based upon the Appellate Division decision
> and the gubernatorial commutation the State
> believes that it would be a waste of both
> judicial and prosecutorial resources and
> contrary to the interests of justice to further
> pursue count one of this indictment. For that
> reason, the State requests that count one of
> this indictment be dismissed."

We appealed to the New Jersey Supreme Court immediately, but would find out sixteen months later that they had no interest in hearing my case. Another year and four months of waiting for nothing.

When I finally met Jenna at the baggage claim at Miami International, she could tell I wasn't doing well. She got me back to the hotel and put me in bed, where I stayed for the next few days. I slept for almost two days straight. I had never had a panic attack before. I thought people made them up as an excuse for their inability to deal with the consequences of their own bad decisions.

But there I was, lying in bed in the dark with the curtains blackening out the warmth of the ocean. I was unable to move. I knew there was more fighting to do, but I didn't know who was left to fight. I couldn't believe I had come so far, just to fall short of the end zone.

Many people wondered why Governor Christie commuted my sentence and didn't just pardon me. The answer is simple: I didn't ask him to pardon me, I asked him to commute my sentence. Inmates are given several options when requesting executive clemency: a commutation of sentence would get me out of prison as soon as possible and allow me the opportunity to appeal the convictions, to continue the fight, and to take my case as far as necessary until the wrongs were righted.

Requesting a pardon would have begged the governor to forgive me for a crime I didn't commit. Governor Christie understood the distinction and recognized the principal behind my request—and honored it.

On the cold December morning I was released, my parents, a news crew from a local TV station, and a handful of journalists were waiting outside.

The next day, my ecstatic mother told Jason Nark of *The Daily News*, "I haven't woken up with a smile in a long, long time."

While Nark was at my house for the exclusive I told him I wanted to focus on seeing Logan again.

"That's what this all boils down to. For the last two years, I just wanted to be my son's father," I told Nark from behind the poinsettias on my parents' kitchen table. "I'm looking forward to spending the next couple of days on the phone with anyone who can help me see my son again. This is not over."

I filed a motion in family court to reinstate my visitation and to contest the tens of thousands of dollars in fees and arrears they had levied against me while I was in prison. The judge ruled against me on all counts. He didn't seem to care that the governor had intervened on my behalf. I still couldn't see my son. With those unjustifiable fees levied against me, the Department of State revoked my passport and I've been trapped in a country that doesn't respect my autonomy as an individual. Not free to live here. Not free to live anywhere else.

Somehow, I feel like Christie's help did more harm than good in Judge Franklin's courtroom. My conservative values were never welcomed in there, and becoming the poster boy for Second Amendment rights didn't do me any good.

Lea didn't even show up.

It didn't help that some media outlets were sensationalizing the truth in order to score cheap clickbait. The consequences —that a judge would perceive me as a dangerous felon toting around "cop-killer" bullets and keep me from my son —didn't seem to carry any weight in their decision to vie for a few extra advertising dollars.

The Trentonian had been sympathetic about my wrongful incarceration while I was imprisoned but, after I was released by Governor Christie and became the de-facto enemy of New Jersey liberalism, they ran a story under the sensational headline *Burlco Gun Lover Wins Commutation of Seven-Year*

Prison Term From Governor.

The opening paragraph said I had "cop-killer bullets."

Unlike *The Trentonian*'s previous article about me, this article went unsigned and was written by anonymous "staff reporters."

I can only assume by "cop-killer bullets" the *Trentonian* "reporters" meant hollow-point bullets, the very bullets cops carry and that are recommended by police commissioners all across the country. Even the flagship of all liberal newspapers, *The New York Times*, had published several articles declaring the responsible choice of hollow-point ammunition for self-defense.

Just before the New York City Police Department became the last major police department to change from ball-point ammo to hollow-point ammo, Police Commissioner Howard Safir told the *Times* "We are, in fact, going to switch to hollow-point ammunition as soon as we receive it. They are much safer than fully jacketed bullets, which will go through a person or tumble through a person's organs and then continue on and hit innocent victims."

A year earlier Dr. Charles Hirsch, the New York medical examiner at the time, told the *Times* "They [hollow-point bullets] do not produce grotesque, devastating injuries and they are much less likely to pierce through a person, a wall, a car or some other object than are fully jacketed bullets. I think they are safer."

The kind of misinformation and half-assed journalism perpetuated in that *Trentonian* article is part of the reason why people are so poorly informed when it comes to the truth about guns and public safety. That inflammatory fear mongering is why we have such stupid laws on the books that turn innocent people into felons just for taking their property from one house to another.

As the months and years passed, I found myself caring less about what other people said. I never cared much in the first place, except that words have consequences. After all, a lie can travel halfway around the world while the truth is still putting on its shoes.

With the dust finally settling, I decided to petition the Supreme Court of the United States (SCOTUS) to do what the New Jersey Supreme Court wouldn't: overturn the last illogical conviction and reverse the appellate divisions reckless decision that potentially turned thousands of law abiding gun owners into felons overnight. SCOTUS only hears about eighty of the ten-thousand cases petitioned to them every year—not even 1%. But I found myself again with nothing left to lose and everything to gain—for myself, for my son, and for anyone who might ever find themselves victim of an unwieldy judge and green-eyed prosecutor.

I was also raising funds to try and get partial custody of my son. With the word spreading through major media outlets across the country, it wasn't long before a friend told me that Lea had taken our son and moved him out West to avoid any court order that might compel her to allow our son to have a relationship with his father.

I wasn't even surprised by her antics anymore. Worse, I knew she wouldn't face any repercussions for moving him thousands of miles away without my consent.

All of my emails, phone calls, and messages through friends to her went unanswered. Every time I filed a motion in court the judge ruled against me and I wound up sanctioned thousands of dollars, worse off than I was before. I don't have the tens-of-thousands of dollars I need to retain a diligent family-law attorney and, until I do, I continue to dig my hole deeper by representing myself. Even though she's never worked a day in her life she's able to finance a lawyer with her trust fund and my child-support payments. She'd bankrupt me before ever letting me take my son for a hike in the mountains or teach him how to ski.

In my sleep, I sometimes see myself picking him up for the weekend. Lea and I smile at each other. We're not quite friends, but we both love our son and do what's best for him. We do a good job tolerating each other's company. She's moved on and we're able to have dinner together with our son and our new significant others. It's a portrait of the modern American family.

But then I wake up.

Jenna was there for all of it. She kept me from forgetting who I was before all of this started—before the orange jumpsuits and sensational headlines. She reminded me of the times when we could just be each other, and simply be *with* each other. She was everything a husband could possibly want in a wife and, two months after that trip to Miami, I asked her to marry me.

We were wed in a small ceremony with friends and family in the Green Mountains of Vermont. It was a beautiful January day with the sun reflecting off the snow-covered hills. We ate carrot-spice cake with maple icing and called it a "mouthful of Vermont." We danced into the early hours of the next morning. Everything was perfect and everyone was there.

Everyone but one, that is.

I had hoped Lea and I would have enough of a relationship that Logan might be able to be at my wedding. Perhaps he could even be the ring-bearer. But she continued her campaign to cause me pain at the expense of our son.

I wouldn't even know what he looked like—or that he was even still alive—if it weren't for a mutual acquaintance who secretly sends me photos of him.

As far as the Ocean County Family Court is concerned, I am a deadbeat father who wants nothing to do with his son. That isn't true, and never has been. I think about him every single day and miss him in ways our language hasn't evolved to explain.

The sun was setting over Sloan Kettering Hospital when the nurse came back in. She'd been coming to check in on Jenna every hour. She took her blood pressure and checked her vitals as Jenna slowly woke through the fog of her medication.

Together, the nurse and I cleaned her surgical incisions, checked her drains, and replaced her bandages. The dryness of the hospital left Jenna's lips chapped, and I held water up to her lips for her to drink. While the nurse administered another push of painkillers into Jenna's bloodstream, Jenna deliriously told her how we had just been married three and a half months ago.

"Well, you get to go through the challenging times first," the nurse said as she gave us both a practiced smile.

Jenna and I just looked at each other.

"Thank you," I said finally, as the nurse walked away.

If she only knew.

AFTERWORD

On May 27, 2014 the Supreme Court of the United States denied to hear the authors case, upholding a decision that incriminates thousands of otherwise law-abiding gun owners in New Jersey.

As of writing, it has been 1,936 days since the author was last allowed to see his son.

ORDER FOR COMMUTATION OF SENTENCE

WHEREAS, Brian D. Aitken was convicted of Possession of Dum-Dum Bullets in the Fourth Degree in violation of N.J.S.A 2C:39-3(f)(1), Possession of Large Capacity Ammunition Magazine in the Fourth Degree in violation of N.J.S.A 2C:39-3(j), and Unlawful Possession of a Handgun in the Second Degree in violation of N.J.S.A 2C:39-5(b) in the Superior Court, Law Division (Criminal), Burlington County, New Jersey, and was sentenced on August 27, 2010 under Indictment No. 09-03-00217-I to a seven-year term of imprisonment with a three-year mandatory minimum; and

WHEREAS, the said Brian D. Aitken, caused to be made a written application to the Governor for a Commutation of Sentence for the aforesaid crimes of which he was convicted, and the State Parole Board, upon request of the Governor in accordance with the law, has made an investigation of the facts and circumstances concerning said application for a Commutation of Sentence;

NOW, THEREFORE, I, CHRIS CHRISTIE, Governor of the State of New Jersey by virtue of the authority conferred upon me by the Constitution of New Jersey and the statutes of this State, do hereby grant to the said Brian D. Aitken, a commutation of the aforesaid sentence to time served, and satisfied on December 20, 2010.

IT IS FURTHER ORDERED, that Brian D. Aitken's release from the custody of the New Jersey Department of Corrections be effected as soon as administratively possible, or within a reasonable period to allow for release processing pursuant to customary policy and procedure.

This Order is subject to revocation at any time, at the discretion of the Governor, without notice.

IN TESTIMONY WHEREOF I have hereunto set my hand and caused the Great Seal of the State to be affixed at Trenton this 20th day of December, two thousand-ten.

CHRIS CHRISTIE
GOVERNOR

By the Governor

SECRETARY OF STATE

ACKNOWLEDGEMENTS

This book would not have been possible without the time and toil of several people, for whom the following words are too little to adequately thank.

Firstly, I would like to thank Richard Gilbert, Evan Nappen, and Lou Nappen for their masterful work representing me at trial, in a very successful appeal, and in my petition to the Supreme Court of the United States. You are all first class gentlemen and masters of the law, but of course, you know this already. I would also like to extend my gratitude to Wayne LaPierre, the National Rifle Association (NRA), and each of the individual 4.5 million members of the NRA for stepping in and funding my legal battles when my own funds ran dry.

There were many people and organizations who provided small gestures of support, whom I do not know by name, but who are deserving of my unyielding gratitude. I understand over a hundred thousand strangers called Governor Chris Christie and signed petitions requesting my pardon. You are nameless heroes and without you I am certain this story would have a different ending. I would also like to thank Lawrence Reed of the Foundation for Economic Education for hiring me immediately out of prison and for telling donors "we don't leave one of our own wounded on the battlefield." Without your generosity, walking back into the real world would have been far more difficult than it already was.

On a personal level, very little of this memoir would have been possible without the constant support of my friends and family. They have had to endure a great deal already, and writing this book forced many to relive moments of the past we'd all prefer to forget.

I could fill another two hundred pages with words of thanks for my parents but I know, even then, the words would insufficiently repay my debts. The same is true for my best friend, Michael, his mother, Diane, and my wife's parents, Barbara and Neil.

Writing this book took the better part of ten months and seemed, at first, an impossible task. It would have remained impossible without the help of my writing coach, Tom McCarthy, my editor Nils Parker, and my dust jacket designer Keith Hayes who all collaborated intensely with me to ensure my vision was met. I would be remiss if I did not also mention Patrick Waters for introducing me to *The Ballad of Reading Gaol*, the inspiration for this book's title.

There are three additional people of significance I would like to thank individually.

Dennis Malloy, for being responsible for more than his humility allows him to take credit for.

Governor Chris Christie for putting his neck on the line for a kid from South Jersey he'd never even met.

And for Jenna. My editing coach, best friend, and muse. Who could ask for more?

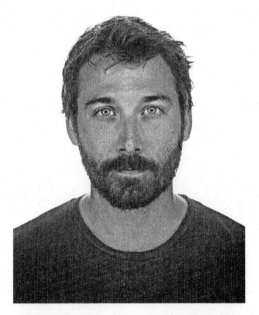

BRIAN D. AITKEN

Mr. Aitken lives in a small mountain hamlet outside the artistic college town of New Paltz, NY with his wife Jenna and two dogs: Frankenstein and Rockefeller. When not at home he can be found ice-climbing in the Rocky Mountains or hiking in the Adirondack's.

You can find him on Twitter at @briandaitken, or on Facebook at www.facebook.com/thebrianaitken

www.briandaitken.com

CPSIA information can be obtained at www.ICGtesting.com
Printed in the USA
BVOW09*2118101114

374462BV00005BA/12/P